Straightening out the
self-centred church

Straightening out the self-centred church

The message of Titus

John Benton

EVANGELICAL PRESS

EVANGELICAL PRESS
12 Wooler Street, Darlington, Co. Durham, DL1 1RQ, England

First published 1997

British Library Cataloguing in Publication Data available

ISBN 0 85234 384 1

Printed and bound in Great Britain at the Bath Press, Bath

To Ann,
the one and only

Christianity as St Paul thinks of it is a great venture. It is a venture staked upon the eternal future. It bids men lay out of their time, and dispose of their lives, and order their daily action on the supposition — the tremendous supposition, which it takes as certain — that this life is but a preface, and a very short preface, to another, and an endless life that will follow. And the warrant for doing this is that Christ is risen from the dead.

H. P. Liddon

Contents

Preface

The idea behind this book was set off by some comments concerning the failings of the post-modern church in Western society, in a stimulating little booklet by Brian J. Walsh entitled *Subversive Christianity*. He spoke of a gap in modern Christians' lives between their world-view and their way of life which would not be bridged simply by more good intentions and more fervent commitment to Christ. Christians are being subverted by contemporary culture in ways of which they are hardly aware.

I took up this idea in a New Year's message at the beginning of 1994, and from the response I realized I was touching on a very definite problem for many in the congregation. It was as if I had voiced for us all something that we had been struggling to understand about ourselves for some time. The next few months were spent in trying to define and grasp more clearly the problem of how the contemporary world around us affects, almost unconsciously, the way we think. In the midst of this I recognized that many of the problems of the contemporary church were similar to those faced by Titus on the island of Crete when Paul wrote to him about the churches there. The present-day church's vulnerability to false teachers, the issues of the roles of men and women, the despising of authority and the general 'me-centred' attitudes which go together in our times also went together in the churches of first-century Crete. Why should that be?

Eventually what I had begun to understand about the problem of the gap in contemporary Christian life emerged through a series of Sunday morning expositions at Chertsey Street, in the autumn of 1994, from Paul's epistle to Titus. It is these sermons which form the basis of this Welwyn commentary.

I have used books and ideas from a number of different preachers and writers in attacking my subject and I hope they will not mind me raiding their larders. Especial mention should be given to Roy Clements' lecture to the UCCF in 1994. Along with Brian Walsh and the work of Os Guiness, this helped to clarify many issues for me.

I must thank Eileen Savage, who has once again worked so hard in putting the notes of this computer-illiterate pastor through the word processor and producing a beautifully readable manuscript.

Also, of course, I must thank the leaders and congregation at Chertsey Street Baptist Church, Guildford. We do not pretend to be the best church in the world, we have many faults and failings, but as far as I am concerned to be pastor and preacher to Chertsey Street is a wonderful privilege. It is a greater privilege than this poor sinner deserves to be part of such a lovely part of God's family. I love the church. May the Lord watch over us, use us, keep us and protect us from all Satan's devices, old or new.

John Benton
Chertsey Street,
Guildford
January 1997

Introduction

Crete is a mainly mountainous, but beautiful island sitting some sixty miles south-east of Greece in the sunny Mediterranean Sea. It is about 150 miles long (east to west), and varies in breadth (north to south) from thirty-five miles to around seven miles. Many people go there these days for a wonderful sun-drenched holiday.

But for Titus Crete was no holiday. It was while he had been left on the island of Crete that he received his letter from the apostle Paul during the early days of Christianity. The Christian faith may well have touched the island quite early in the outreach of the church, for Acts 2 records for us the fact that there were people from Crete present on the Day of Pentecost when the Holy Spirit was first poured out on the church in Jerusalem by the risen Lord Jesus Christ (Acts 2:11). However, it seems it was some time later that churches were properly established in the island. It was probably after his first imprisonment in Rome that Paul had made an apostolic visit to the island and planted churches. But for reasons of which we are no longer aware he was unable to stay very long. So as Paul writes his letter the newly planted churches on the island were churches which needed a lot of straightening out of things left unfinished (1:5). Titus, Paul's friend and junior helper in the gospel, had been left there to get things sorted out.

Unfinished faith

If you take the time to read through this short letter to Titus, it becomes plain that while one of the major tasks for Titus to undertake involved the appointment of leaders/elders (1:5) in the congregations in the different towns in Crete, Paul had a lot more in mind than just that when he spoke about straightening out the things left unfinished. For a start there were false teachers and erroneous teachings to be dealt with (1:9-10). But, more than that, it seems as if there was a sense in which the faith of the Christians in Crete was itself unfinished.

What do I mean? In the very first verse of the letter Paul speaks of the gospel as 'the truth that leads to godliness'. Faith needs to be expressed in fruitful lives for God. But this was not happening as it should among the Cretan Christians. They were not responding well to the fact that the good news of God's grace and love ought to lead us to live a good and godly lifestyle.

You can pick this up in a number of references throughout the letter. Here are three examples. In 2:1 Paul encourages Titus to 'teach what is in accord with sound doctrine', and what he goes on to emphasize in the following verses are certain aspects of practical Christian living for men and women. Presumably, as yet, such practical Christianity had not been forthcoming. Later in the same chapter Paul stresses it plainly: 'The grace of God that brings salvation has appeared to all men. It teaches us to say "No" to ungodliness and worldly passions, and to live self-controlled, upright and godly lives in this present age' (2:11-12). The believing reception of Christian truth ought to issue in distinctively disciplined Christian living. This needed spelling out to the Cretan Christians.

A final example is found in 3:8. Having set out in the preceding verses a wonderful summary of the 'kindness and love of God our Saviour', Paul says to Titus, 'I want you to stress these things, so that those who have trusted in God may be careful to devote themselves to doing what is good.' Evidently devotion to doing good was not happening as it should among the Christians in Crete.

There was a gap between what they professed to believe and the way they actually lived. Does that sound familiar? I suspect that rings bells for many of us in the modern church. Many Christians today, I sense, are uneasily aware that there is a gap between our conscious commitment to the Lord Jesus and the way we live out our lives. We know that in a sense there will always be something of a gap in our lives all the way until we reach heaven. No Christian lives perfectly this side of glory. However, many Christians today are aware that this gap in their lives is far wider than it ought to be. It seems a greater divide than the gap in the lives of Christians of previous generations. Also, strangely, it appears that this gap does not always arise from conscious disobedience to the Lord. Often sincere Christians find that this gap is opening up in their lives and they are rather bewildered by it. They have set themselves to follow harder after Christ, to be more in prayer and searching the Scriptures, and yet this has not brought an immediate solution. Something is happening which they do not quite understand, and they are not sure how to improve!

The gap between belief and behaviour is the central theme of Paul's letter to Titus and it has much to say to our generation of Christians as we stand on the brink of the twenty-first century. Often the letter to Titus is dealt with in Bible commentaries as an afterthought along with 1 and 2 Timothy, under the umbrella description of 'the Pastoral Epistles' as those letters written specifically to Christian workers, rather than first of all to churches. Although this epistle has included ample teaching concerning the conduct of Christian leadership, it is arguable that a more fruitful line of approach to Titus is to pick up from the beginning on this problem of the gap in

Christian living among the churches of Crete. This is the approach we shall adopt in this commentary.

Modern lives

Just consider the problem for a moment. The cause of the gap is always the same. It is the influence on us of the godless society around us. The moulding influence of the contemporary pagan culture has always been the major cause of the sicknesses of the church throughout history. Christians of a previous generation called it the problem of worldliness.

Now we need to be careful not to overreact. Christian involvement in society has positive as well as negative aspects. The world is double-edged. It is God's world. He made it. He sustains it. It therefore has many things for us richly to enjoy (1 Tim. 4:4; 6:17). But, of course, it is also a fallen world and the devil's stronghold, and therefore it is a place of danger. Again, on the positive side, if Christians become too cloistered and detached from society, we forfeit the contact and ability to share the gospel with a lost world. If we shut ourselves away we cannot obey Christ's command to take the good news into all the world. But once more negatively, we can become involved with the world in a way that compromises us, and the world subverts the way we live and a yawning chasm opens up between what we say we stand for and how we live it out. So the world must be handled carefully.

The dominating characteristic of modern life, compared with previous centuries, is the pace of change. In travel, trade, technological advance, the spread of ideas, our world moves at breathtaking speed. The problem with the modern church is often not that we lack understanding of Christian basics, or that our sinful nature is somehow worse than that of believers in other centuries (it has always been bad!). Our problem is that in our fast-changing modern world the culture has moved on and is often subverting us in ways we have not yet caught up with or realized. Hence mere rededication is sometimes not enough. Very often the thinking of average Christians is actually too far behind the times for them to identify how the world is attacking their souls.

Let me quote a story from the writer Os Guiness. It is a story from the old Soviet Union. Lots of items were being stolen from a joinery factory in the old USSR by the workers. So a guard was put on the gate. On the first night that the Communist guard was there, out comes Petrovich with a suspicious-looking sack on a wheelbarrow. 'What have you got?' asks the guard. 'It's just woodshavings,' replies Petrovich. The guard shouts, 'All right, tip it out!' Sure enough it was just woodshavings, and so the guard let him pass. This happened night after night, and the guard knew there was something going on, but he could not figure it out. Eventually he was so annoyed and intrigued that he got hold of Petrovich and said, 'I know you are up to something and it's driving me mad. Tell me and I'll let you go. What are you stealing?' Petrovich smiled and answered, 'Wheelbarrows!'

Sadly the laugh is on evangelical Christians. While we have set up guards to keep Sunday special and be anti-abortion and anti-homosexual practice and on the alert for any deviations from sound doctrine (all very necessary and good things), the devil has been trundling far more subtle things into our lives by the back door, which if we are not careful will eventually lead us to fold on the other issues anyway. What those subtle things are specifically we shall be trying to highlight as we go through Titus. But if you wanted one word to sum up, it would be 'subjectivism'.

Cretan character

The people of Crete in those early days of Christianity were known as a self-centred lot. Paul quotes a comment by a sixth-century B.C. Cretan author. Epimenides, on the character of his fellow-countrymen: 'Cretans are always liars, evil brutes, lazy gluttons' (1:12). Evidently six centuries later they were still the same. It is a generalization and must be taken as such, but nevertheless it seems quite plain that Cretans had a reputation for being aggressively subjective in their outlook. Polybius, another ancient writer, says, 'Greed and avarice are so native to the soil of Crete, that they are the only people among whom no stigma attaches to any sort of gain whatever.' They would do anything for self.

Subjectivism and aggression do not always go together, but often they do. If people see themselves and their feelings as the centre of the universe then insensitivity to others is not too far away, and hostility towards others is only a step beyond that.

The reasons for this tempestuous subjective trend in the Cretan personality are perhaps impossible to track down. Lying in the middle of the Mediterranean between Europe, Asia and Africa, Crete was from earliest times something of a stepping-stone between the continents. Oriental ideas and religions met there with the philosophies of Greece. The heyday of Crete, Minoan civilization, was back around 2200-1500 B.C. and was famed for its mythical King Minos. Fishing was the basis for the Minoan economy. It was a prosperous and rich culture. The Minoans built huge palaces, such as the palace at Knossos, their main city. King Minos was supposed to be the owner of the Labyrinth, a warren of tunnels in which lived the fabled Minotaur, a monster with the body of a man and the head of a bull which fed on human flesh. He doesn't sound like too much of a sensitive mortal, does he? After a volcanic eruption on the nearby island of Thera in about 1550

B.C. peoples from mainland Greece overran Crete and the civilization of the Minoans went into decline. The great culture had failed, leaving people disorientated. Also Crete was a recruiting ground for mercenary troops who travelled to and from distant battles in faraway places. These men too would have brought back a hotch-potch of ideas about religion and life, as Crete fell into decline.

When people are confused about life and there seem to be no well-understood answers to life's ultimate questions, then subjectivism and a philosophy of 'looking after number one' is the only idea that makes sense. Perhaps the labyrinth myth itself reflected the confusion and the tragedy of life felt by the Cretans.

In the centuries running up to the coming of Christ, the island became the haunt of pirates, and Crete was divided among a number of feuding city-states until it was subdued by Rome in 67 B.C. These too may have been influences on breeding a materialistic, aggressive self-centredness into the people of Crete.

Post-modern people

They must not be pressed too far, but there are parallels between the self-centredness of Crete and the subjectivism which dominates our society at the close of the twentieth century. We too belong to a civilization that shows signs of being in decline. The Enlightenment vision of the eighteenth century of a modern world governed by reason and science has not brought a happy, stable society. The vision has failed.

We have gone beyond the romanticism which arose and flourished in the Victorian era and the beginning of this century, with its emphasis on noble feelings and emotions. Our 'gods' have failed. We have retreated further into ourselves.

We are now in the world of post-modernism which proclaims that there is no reality at all for the individual except subjective reality. The only thing of any importance is individual freedom and the way the individual perceives the world. Whatever it takes, we just want to feel good.

The lack of any generally accepted values or purpose in life leaves contemporary people disorientated with nothing but 'to do what is right in their own eyes'. The constant pressures of modern life, with its continuing demands and hassles, and the need to have everything done quickly and if possible by yesterday, forces people into subjectivism: 'I've got no time to think what life is about; I have enough problems just making sure I survive each day.' In a host of different ways 1990s' people have come to a Narcissus-like obsession with themselves and their rights and their feelings. Personal organizers, personal space, personal development, personal therapies and personal assertiveness are the names of the game.

Of course, the subtlety of all this is that biblically this is half valid. God does care for us as individuals. The very hairs of our heads are numbered. But almost unconsciously the subjective mindset has totally taken over our lives. We are only interested in God being there for us. Like someone looking through a pair of tinted spectacles we view everything in life in terms of the question: 'How does this affect me?' However, once we are wearing tinted spectacles everything tends to look the same colour. We are not too good at distinguishing blue from green. Once everything is coming to us through the filter of 'How does this affect me?' or 'How does this make me feel?' then we are in bad shape to distinguish any truth from lies, for sometimes the truth hurts and the lie is comforting. With our glasses of subjectivism firmly in place we are badly placed to differentiate between right and wrong. What is right and what is wrong? Right becomes just what is good for me. Wrong is similarly self-centred. And all this inevitably affects our relationship with God. We are fundamentally out of step with the God of objective truth and holiness.

The subjectivist even begins to read the Bible in a different way. We no longer read it as a book of history, or a covenant promise of life to inform us of the truth. Rather for many it has become a kind of personal spiritual horoscope from which we get our own temporary thrill. What Scripture is saying to our minds is set aside for the quick fix of comfort it can give to our emotions. Once we are into such an outlook concerning our spirituality then principled Christian living is nowhere. The gap in our lives opens up.

Just as the aggressive self-centredness of Crete was ruining the outworking of Christian faith in Titus' day, so the subjectivism of our day is ruining our walk with God, and opening up an even wider chasm between what we say we believe and how we actually behave.

As Paul writes to Titus, he is well aware of the problem. But he has a sure and firm answer. It is Paul's answer which will more than suffice for us today as we look at the ills of the Christian community at the end of the twentieth century. The apostle provides us with spiritual dynamite to blast a way out of the prison of subjectivism into the freedom and integrity which is ours in Christ.

Titus is not just a book for trainee pastors, elders and Christian leaders. It is a book which has an urgent message for us all.

1.
Why the truth matters!

Please read Titus 1:1-4

The most influential image of our modern world is that of a market-place. For many people this description pictures most clearly the way the world works and how its people interact, not just in matters of trade, but in all kinds of relationships.

Over the last quarter of the twentieth century much of our life as people and nations has been rearranged in conformity to this image. Many traditional ways of handling matters have gone. Everything from education to health is now seen in terms of products, consumers and prices. We speak of market forces, market research, market value. This is our culture.

Behind this image of the market-place there is a philosophy. At the centre of the market is the idea of the sanctity of individual choice. True freedom is for the individual to stroll through life's bazaar, stopping at the different stalls and making his or her own selection. The market is therefore an image which promotes a subjective attitude to life. The philosophy behind the market-place is one which idolizes the freedom of individuals to choose whatever they think is best for them. The centre of the market is really the self and its perceived needs.

The driving force of the market-place is competition between the different traders. They must contend with one another in an ever-changing battle to grab attention and market-share. The market-place is a very temporal affair. Fashions change. The whims of the customers are in continual flux. It is very much rooted in the here and now. The trader who can somehow produce what the individual finds most instantly attractive at the most competitive price, while still making a profit, is king in the market-place. This is a view of the world which many people would see as most realistic.

But, as Christians, we need to be reminded that this is not the Bible's image of the way the world should ultimately be seen. According to Scripture, the world is not finally a market-place, but a kingdom belonging to God. As Christians living in a self-centred world we need to reflect seriously on this. The driving force of a kingdom is not that of the competition of rival merchants, but the power of an unrivalled kingly throne. The centre of a kingdom is ultimately not freedom of choice for the individual, but the will of the sovereign. A kingdom is described by a completely different set of words from a market. These words are not words like preferences, alternatives and options. They are words like authority, obligation, loyalty, submission and calling.

The Cretan Christians' fundamental trouble was that of a vast gap between what they said they believed and how they actually behaved. In today's Western society the church generally suffers from the very same gap, and one of the main reasons behind that gap is that Christians have been subverted by the cult of self. The market mentality contributes to that cult.

There is the market and the kingdom. We find ourselves torn between these two very different ways of looking at the world and more than we realize we have been subverted by an outlook on life which, although superficially it seems to contain much realism, is actually self-centred and is not ultimately the biblical outlook.

The letter to Titus is a letter which tackles the problem of living as Christians in a self-centred culture. As Paul begins his letter it is very striking how his opening remarks profoundly reflect the absolute kingship of God, and by implication challenge the whole atmosphere of subjectivism which dominated the ethos of first-century Crete, and dominates our post-modern Western culture today: **'Paul, a servant of God, and an apostle of Jesus Christ for the faith of God's elect and the knowledge of the truth that leads to godliness — a faith and knowledge resting on the hope of eternal life, which God, who does not lie, promised before the beginning of time, and at his appointed season he brought his word to light through the preaching entrusted to me by the command of God our Saviour, to Titus, my true son in our common faith: grace and peace from God the Father and Christ Jesus our Saviour.'**

In confronting the gap, do you see where Paul starts? He immediately lifts our eyes above this world, its temporary fads and values, and begins by directing our thoughts to the sovereign God and the objective reality of eternal life which God desires people to have. What he is ultimately doing is lifting our attention to see that there is a King in heaven, and there is a heavenly lifestyle (he calls it 'godliness', 1:1) here on earth which cuts across the prevalent cultures. It is a way of living which is never out of date. It is distinct from the ways of the world, because it flows from God's throne and is the present expression of that eternal life which has about it all the beauty, gravity and joy of God himself.

Let us see how Paul brings these things out. The introductory verses can be subsumed under three headings. These are Paul's calling, Paul's responsibility and Paul's greeting.

Paul's calling (1:1)

'Paul, a servant of God and an apostle of Jesus Christ for the faith of God's elect and the knowledge of the truth that

leads to godliness.' Paul introduces himself uniquely here, in the first verse of Titus, as God's servant. To people who see the world as revolving around themselves, Paul's emphasis on God and his service should come as a thunderclap. He is not talking of one god among many from whom we may choose. He is talking of the reality of the one true God to whom we are all answerable. God is the great destroyer of the purely subjective outlook on life. There is someone in the universe far more important than you or I. There is someone who reigns, who created us and to whom we must give an account. There is someone whose very existence shatters totally the idea that truth and morality are merely relative values or personal choice. There is someone who overturns the stalls of the market-traders in our lives. There is a God before whom we must stand in submissive awe.

Flying in an aircraft is not something I particularly enjoy. I have on occasion travelled to the U.S. and to Africa in a jumbo jet. To sit by the window of the aircraft and look down and see New York harbour like a small map below you, and to realize the immense distance you are flying above the earth and what it would be like to fall out of the plane, is awesome. We are sobered, even terrified, by the thought. And height is just one of the metaphors the Bible uses to convey to us the awesomeness of God. 'As the heavens are higher than the earth, so are my ways higher than your ways and my thoughts than your thoughts,' says God. He is, in his very being, 'the Most High', who says, 'Heaven is my throne, and the earth is my footstool.' If we are awed by mere vertical distance when we fly in a plane, how much more should we be awed by the spiritual and moral distance between ourselves and the sovereign God! The Christian message begins with the fact of God — God without comparison, or competitor, or rival, whom we dare not treat like so many goods in a market.

A servant of God

Paul is God's servant. The phrase has an Old Testament background in that the prophets were often designated 'servants of God'. Paul, too, in a special way is God's spokesman. But his servanthood reflects God's position. God is the King. Paul is a man whose own will is bowed before the will of God. He has laid down his choices at the King's feet. He is committed, not to pleasing himself, but to faithful service as a slave to a gracious Master. Paul's life revolves around the Lord.

The self-centred attitude of the market-place will ultimately fail us, for it is not founded in the reality of God. The market-place is about making our choices, getting what we want. But as I go through life more and more I meet people who say, 'When I get what I want I find it isn't what I want.' Having our own way produces only a transitory elation, but leaves us empty. 'What was the point?' we eventually ask ourselves. We satiate our desires to no purpose. Without God we are like ships without anchors. We are like travellers who never reach home. The truth is that we were made for God, and we can never find true satisfaction outside his loving service. 'Take my yoke upon you and learn from me,' said Jesus, '... and you will find rest for your souls' (Matt. 11:29). We can only find our roots in submission to the sovereign God.

An apostle of Christ

Paul next adds further detail to his calling by speaking of himself as Christ's apostle. God reveals himself graciously to us through the Lord Jesus Christ. To serve Christ is to serve God. On the road to Damascus the risen Lord Jesus Christ revealed himself to Paul in his glory. There and then the Lord

Jesus had made Paul an apostle. The word 'apostle' means someone who has been selected and sent personally by the risen Lord Jesus Christ with Christ's own authority delegated to him. Paul's calling, therefore, is to be, along with the other apostles, the link between God and ourselves.

The faith of God's elect

This commission from the Lord Jesus leads us immediately to the third element of which Paul speaks as he describes his calling. Paul tells us the purpose for which he is God's servant and Christ's apostle. The object of Paul's service is **'for the faith of God's elect and the knowledge of the truth that leads to godliness'**. Paul is an apostle with the purpose of bringing people to know God through faith in Christ.

The phrase 'the faith of God's elect' has both a backward and a forward reference. With respect to the past, Old Testament Israel were known as God's elect, the chosen people. By using this phrase concerning his ministry, Paul is first of all establishing the fact that his ministry and the Christian faith he preaches are not things which have sprung up out of nowhere. They are continuous with God's work since time began, and embrace the future outworking of his eternal plans in the world. Indeed, Paul is going to go on, in verse 2, to explain his work in relation to what God 'promised before the beginning of time'. The world's markets may rise and fall, its fashions may come and go, but there is a continuous work of God going on in the world and Paul is part of it.

The phrase 'the faith of God's elect' also has a forward reference. It points to Paul's preaching and evangelism. It is telling us that those who come to saving faith in the Lord Jesus Christ are the elect, the chosen of God. The mention of the sovereign election of individuals to salvation by God is another lightning bolt striking at the heart of man-centred

subjectivism prevalent in Cretan culture. When people become Christians they do choose Christ. But behind their
choice is the prior choice of God. As we shall see later, this
truth is actually a tremendous encouragement to lost sinners,
but initially it is a truth which humbles us to the dust. It wrecks
our autonomous mentality about life. It is not that we choose
God, but that he chooses us. Our destiny is not ultimately in our
own hands, but in the hands of God. We are not the prime
movers in the world; God is. Paul is called by God to bring his
elect to saving faith.

But then notice how Paul goes on to describe that faith. He
calls it 'the knowledge of the truth that leads to godliness'. The
two vital emphases are on truth and godliness.

Truth

In first-century Crete, as today, with lots of religious ideas
around and a very subjective 'feel-good' attitude dominating
the general outlook, when someone like Paul talks about 'the
truth' people dispute that there is such a thing. 'You call it the
truth,' they say, 'but it's just your opinion. What is true for you
might not be true for me.' 'Truth' for them is just what happens
to make them 'feel good' or bring some immediate subjective
advantage.

How do we answer such people? Well, first, we should
point out that a thoroughgoing subjectivism is actually self-
defeating. If subjective opinion is the only thing that exists on
any topic, then there is eventually no point in talking. Commu-
nication is actually impossible, because you can only ever
have your own opinion, and you can never know if what you
subjectively heard someone else say was really what he or she
meant. And, of course, you cannot check to find out, for when
you do, you can never be sure that the other person heard your
question in the way you meant it, or that you heard the answer

with anything more than your own subjective interpretation. Pure subjectivism leads logically to silence. It is a non-starter.

Secondly, we must point out that although people may engage in convoluted philosophical arguments about the existence of objective truth, nobody actually lives life as if there were no such thing. It is not an open question as to whether two plus two equals four. It is objective truth. It is the same for everyone. It is not a matter of opinion that a teaspoon of arsenic kills. It is objective truth, and if you try to live as if this were not true, you soon forfeit life! The world is not all a matter of opinion. The truth exists.

But in contending for truth, thirdly we must point such people to the facts of Christianity. Living in the TV age, we have become desensitized to history. We foolishly think that unless we can see something on a screen then it did not happen, as if reality only began when TV was invented. But, of course, the facts of history stand. The nation of Israel in the Old Testament and the existence of the church now are facts, consequences of God's activity in history. Paul has spoken of 'God's elect' and the great story of God's dealings with his people down the ages is recorded for us faithfully in the book of Scripture. Furthermore, God's book is a self-authenticating book. Its Old Testament predictions, written hundreds and sometimes thousands of years in advance, have been fulfilled in Jesus Christ. He has come and died for our sins and risen again according to the Scriptures. The course of history itself has been changed by his coming. Paul himself was an eyewitness of the risen Lord Jesus. The facts are plain. The truth stands. And it stands whether it makes us feel good or not. Truth is not a market commodity. It will not cease to be the truth if you don't choose to buy it. It will not become false if you choose to ignore it and leave it on the shelf. God is there whether we like it or not. This is why the truth matters.

Godliness

The second vital emphasis is on godliness. The gospel is **'the truth that leads to godliness'**.

In today's world of markets and consumers, godliness is probably the last thing that people want. They see their needs in terms of personal well-being or personal fulfilment and satisfaction, not costly godly living. Yet this is because, viewing the world through the spectacles of subjectivism, people fail to perceive their true need.

The word translated here 'godliness' 'denotes that piety', says W. E. Vine, 'which, characterized by a Godward attitude, does that which is well-pleasing to Him'. Here is yet another bombshell against self-centredness. When the gospel is rightly received into our lives it is productive of godliness. The inevitable consequence will be a definite turning of our backs on subjectivism and self-centredness, and definite strides taken towards pleasing God, who is now the centre of our lives. Unless such a change is taking place in our lives then we have no sincere faith, we have no genuine knowledge and love of the truth. Godliness is the mark that we truly have been saved. This is why Paul is so concerned about the churches on Crete, and would have a similar concern over so much that passes as Christianity today.

The phrase 'the truth that leads to godliness' has another side to it. The churches on Crete faced many false teachers, as is evident later in the letter. But false teaching can never produce godliness. Godliness is embodied in, and communicated through, the truths of the faith concerning the Lord Jesus Christ. If the truth is polluted or replaced by error then inevitably godliness will not ensue. Godliness is a flower which comes only from the seed of truth. This is why the truth is so important. Our greatest need is not to select the religion which most suits us from the bazaar of world beliefs. Rather it is to receive the truth which leads to godliness.

Paul's responsibility (1:2-3)

Having summarized his calling, Paul now explains in more detail the importance of his own ministry. As Christ's apostle he further describes the faith he is charged with preaching as **'a faith and knowledge resting on the hope of eternal life, which God, who does not lie, promised before the beginning of time, and at his appointed season he brought his word to light through the preaching entrusted to me by the command of God our Saviour'**.

The hope

The faith which Paul is charged with propagating rests on the hope of eternal life. The word 'hope' refers to the future. When we think of the future we are often uncertain. 'I hope I get the job,' we say before the interview, or 'I hope we have good weather on holiday,' we say as we set off. We use the word 'hope' to refer to things in the future we would like, but of which we are not sure. But biblical hope has an entirely different quality about it. It is a future which is certain because, as we shall see later, it is based on the promise of God who is entirely faithful.

The hope is certain. Central to Paul's message was the fact that the Lord Jesus Christ is risen from the dead. Having died for our sins, he has opened the door into the future for us. The Lord Jesus has opened the door into the realm of eternity in God's glorious presence. As the dying Jesus was able to promise the thief on the cross, 'I tell you the truth, today you will be with me in paradise,' so the soul of every dying believer is received into heaven. As the Lord Jesus rose from death on the third day, so every Christian will be raised bodily on the last day and ushered into 'a new heaven and a new earth, the home of righteousness'.

Our post-modern outlook on life is really an outlook of despair. The hopes people had that the modern world of reason, science and free expression would produce a better world for all are fading under the harsh realities of a disintegrating Western society and life and death at the end of the twentieth century. People have lost their vision. As the Cretans of the first century were the children of Minoan civilization that had failed, so we are the children of a civilization which has lost its way. Once we have lost the vision, selfishness and subjectivism seem to be the only path in life which makes any sense.

But there is another way. The Utopian dreams and kingdoms of men were always built on crumbling foundations. Paul preaches the truth that leads to godliness. He preaches a faith **'resting on the hope of eternal life'**. Here is the cure for despair. Here is a kingdom that will not fade or fail.

The words of Jim Eliot, the American missionary who was killed in South America during the 1950s as he tried to evangelize the Auca Indians, are ever true. He said, 'He is no fool who gives what he cannot keep, to gain what he cannot lose.' This is logic which the market-minded generation of today should ponder! We cannot keep this life. We cannot avoid death. But through faith in Jesus Christ we are given life which is eternal.

The promise — god ﬀ

Eternal life is certain, because it has been promised and provided by God. Paul makes sure that we do not miss the fact that God is faithful. The hope of eternal life was **'promised before the beginning of time'** by **'God, who does not lie'**.

In a subjective, self-centred culture, to tell a lie is often felt to be advantageous. If your only basis for ethics is to do 'what's best for me', then why not? The Cretans, as Paul points out later, were renowned for their lying (1:12). By contrast, the promise of eternal life comes from God who does not lie (Num. 23:19; 1 Sam. 15:29).

We sometimes use the word 'pseudo' to mean something which is imitation, or deceptive, not the real thing. The word Paul uses here of God is *'apseudo'*. He is the antithesis of anything pseudo. He deals exclusively in what is genuine. He does not lie. He cannot lie.

How is it that God is like this? Firstly, because his truthfulness is part of his holiness. God is utterly just and righteous. His nature is such that he cannot go against that, and to lie or deceive is unholy and unjust. Secondly, God is truth and does not lie, because one of the great attributes of truth is that it is always consistent with reality. God is the foundation of reality, the upholder of the universe, and a lie does not match reality. Thirdly, Scripture tells us that the devil is the father of lies (John 8:44). For God to lie would be for him to take the devil's path, and that is impossible. That is why God does not lie. That is why we can trust his promise.

Furthermore, the fact that God does not lie has been proved over and over again in Bible history. God promised Noah that the flood of judgement was coming. And it came. God does not lie. God promised childless Abraham that he would have descendants who would be a great nation. Isaac was born and Israel was the consequence. God does not lie. God said to Moses that he would rescue the Israelites from the bondage of Egypt. Following the plagues on Egypt, Pharaoh let them go. God was not lying. Most of all God's truthfulness and reliability are proved by the sending of the Lord Jesus Christ. This is particularly in Paul's mind here as he thinks about the **'appointed season'** for the gospel being preached to the world.

The coming of Jesus underlines the faithfulness of God. The promise of the Saviour, decided before the beginning of time, was first revealed to fallen Adam and Eve in Eden: the woman's offspring would crush the serpent's head (Gen. 3:15). Though that promise was made so long ago, God had not forgotten it. Christ came. God is faithful.

The promise was made to the most undeserving of people — to us, sinners who have rebelled and offended God endlessly. Yet God does not renege on his promises even when he has every reason to do so. The promise God made was so costly. Who can understand what it meant for God the Father to give his one and only, his beloved Son, over to the toils and temptations of earth, to the pain and wrath of death at Calvary? Yet God did not change his mind. Jesus came.

What God had decided, in his own private councils before time began, he has brought about in Christ. We are reminded again that it is not ultimately our choices which shape and direct history. He rules. He brings to pass all he has promised. And what he lovingly promises is eternal life for sinners. Christian faith rests on the certainty of eternal life promised by God who never lies.

The preaching

We understand the full significance and weight of Paul's responsibility as we realize that Christ having completed his work, Paul and his preaching are now instrumental for the plans of the God of heaven on earth. God, having raised Jesus from the dead and so made good his promise of eternal life, **'at his appointed season ... brought his word to light through the preaching entrusted to me by the command of God our Saviour'**.

Paul has been commanded to preach the Word. He is under obligation. God, the King, has commanded him. Positively, the proclaiming of the truth is the means God uses to bring his elect to faith and to eternal life. Negatively, unless the truth is proclaimed God's purposes that people find eternal life could not be fulfilled.

The story is told that when the world's greatest diamond mines in South Africa came to light in 1866 people were unaware of them. A man called Van Neikerk found stones which looked like diamonds lying about on the ground. He pointed them out. 'Don't be ridiculous,' people said. 'Diamonds in the dust — there to pick up? Don't be a fool!' But Van Neikerk was not put off. He eventually sent one of the stones to a famous geologist, Dr Athertone. The geologist was sceptical at first, but like a true scientist, he did all the tests, and was astonished to find that indeed it was a first-class diamond valued at £500 (which in 1870 was a lot of money!). Van Neikerk and his friend O'Reilly went back to where they had found the diamonds and made an absolute fortune. The diamonds were there all the time, but people passed them by because they did not know the truth about them.

There is a great treasure of eternal life which God desires people to have. He desires it so much that he promised it before time began and gave his Son over to death to secure it. But people will only find it and take it if they know the truth about it.

This is why the truth is precious. By it, people are saved from their sins and given eternal life. The preaching of error cannot do this. Only the truth can do it.

As an apostle, Paul has been sent directly by the Lord Jesus Christ himself. He is an eyewitness of the resurrection. He has received the truth first-hand and has been entrusted with preaching the good news of eternal life to the world.

This is the significance of Paul. This is the responsibility which is laid upon him. This is the sender of this letter.

Paul's greeting

Next we are introduced formally to the person to whom the letter is sent. Obviously the letter is meant to have a wider readership, hence its inclusion in our New Testament, but its initial reader, and the person in mind for whom it was penned was Titus: **'To Titus, my true son in our common faith: grace and peace from God the Father and Christ Jesus our Saviour.'**

From other references in the Scriptures we find that Titus was a close and trusted colleague of the apostle Paul. He accompanied Paul on many of his journeys. He seems to have been a more forceful character than Timothy, and Paul often entrusted crucial tasks to him. Outstanding among these was his delicate mission to Corinth to rescue the tense situation which had arisen between Paul and the Corinthian Christians. This was a task which clearly called for diplomacy as well as integrity. Titus also seems to have been a man with gifts of organization and leadership. He was charged with organizing a collection in Corinth (2 Cor. 8:6). Now Paul had left him in Crete to sort out the problems there (1:5). In many ways we could think of Titus as Paul's faithful troubleshooter.

However, the most pertinent fact for us here is that Titus is a Gentile Greek (Gal. 2:3) and Paul is a Jew. Yet though Titus is a Gentile and Paul is a Jew they are part of the same family. Paul calls Titus his 'true son'. They share a 'common faith' in the Lord Jesus Christ which cuts across the racial and cultural boundaries.

One of the great features of the market of life is competition. There is competition between rich and poor. There is competition between different countries and races. There is competition between the sexes. But in Christ all those barriers come down. What no earthly civilization has achieved down all the years of history has been achieved in Christ. There is neither Jew nor Gentile, but all are one in Christ Jesus.

Paul then pens a benediction to Titus. 'Grace and peace' is Paul's regular form of blessing in most of his letters. Although it has many dimensions to its meaning it is that word 'grace' which is the key to why all racial and cultural distinctions are swept away in Christ.

'Grace' means God's unmerited mercy. Paul wishes Titus to enjoy God's strength and mercy and the spiritual peace which transcends any external circumstances. Such blessings are the birthright of those who belong to God's family through faith in Christ our Saviour. Given the responsibilities with which he is charged and the problems he faces on Crete, he needs God's grace to strengthen him and enable him for the task in hand.

Free grace

Now in fact 'grace', mentioned here in this opening greeting, is at the heart of the good news which Paul preaches. It was because of his free mercy and grace that God the Father sent his Son to be our Saviour. And it is the idea of free grace which gives us a proper understanding of the doctrine of election which Paul has brought to the forefront in these opening verses of his letter. His ministry as an apostle is 'for the faith of God's elect'. It is this same decree of election which makes people all one in Christ Jesus whatever their cultural or social background.

Simply stated, the biblical doctrine of election is that if you or I are Christians, then it is ultimately because God chose us and loved us, back in eternity, long before we ever chose or loved him. God's choice is a gracious choice; that is, it was not made on the basis of any merit or good in us. Neither is it made on the basis of race or cultural background.

On the surface this appears to be a very hard and frightening truth, and indeed it does destroy a self-centred outlook in us completely. We are not the centre of the universe. Ultimately God is in control, not us. It crushes all human arrogance and pride. But apart from this side of the doctrine it is also an extremely positive truth for sinners.

If you could choose who was to be saved, whom would you choose? Perhaps our initial reaction to that question would be to say we would choose everyone. But if everyone without exception were saved, and no one punished for sin, what would have happened to justice? It would look for all the world as if God was indifferent to sin. He would be a judge who let off every offender. So given that you cannot save everyone, ask yourself the question again. If you could choose who was to be saved, whom would you choose?

Imagine all mankind arranged in a vast skyscraper, with the 'good' people at the top and all the ne'er-do-wells and crooks down in the basement. If you chose people to salvation on the basis of 'goodness' then at some level on the skyscraper there would be a cut-off point. Those below the horizontal cut would have no hope. Or suppose you said, 'No, the Bible says people are saved by faith not by goodness, so let's arrange the skyscraper of mankind according to their own faith.' Now all the fresh-faced gullible youngsters would be on the top floor, but the cut-off point would mean there would be no hope for the born cynics in the cellar. Or you could, as the Old Testament Jew perhaps would have thought, arrange mankind according to race, with the Jews at the top and Gentiles below. Or you could arrange people in terms of rich and poor, or any other way you can dream up. But, however you decide to allocate people in the skyscraper, you always end up with at least one group for whom there is no hope. They are below the cut-off point. They are just the wrong type of people.

But the glory of the doctrine of God's gracious election is that it tells us that God's choice is not based on any human categories, and because of that there is hope for all. However we choose to arrange mankind in the skyscraper, however we categorize ourselves, according to whatever criterion, God's 'cut' is always vertical, never horizontal. It cuts through all categories. And therefore no one can ever say, 'I've gone too far,' or 'I'm not the type to be saved,' because there is no 'type' God chooses. It is the doctrine of free grace in unconditional election that means that we can offer hope to everyone. Whoever they are, whatever they have done, whatever their background, the gospel faces people with a simple question: 'Will you have Christ as your Saviour?'

The question people must answer is not, 'Am I one of God's elect?' They can never find out from looking at themselves or the categories other people place them in. The question is rather: 'Will you receive the truth and have Jesus Christ as your Saviour?' If the answer is a sincere 'Yes', then they are among God's elect.

In the market-place people are always contrasting and comparing one another. Who is superior? Who is inferior? Who is only average? For those who are looked upon as second-raters in the market life holds out many hurts. Even those who do scramble to the top of the pile rarely seem to have much joy in it. Who knows when they will fall from their position? But by his sovereign grace God smashes the market. He cuts through all human categories and comparisons.

Paul was a Jew. Titus was a Gentile. But though very different, both were saved through their 'common faith' in the Lord Jesus Christ. Through the preaching of the truth of Jesus Christ, people of every race and language and culture and type come into the possession of eternal life. Are you a saved person? God's grace is wide and free. Why not come to Christ if you have never done so before? God does save people like you. So why not come?

2.
Identikit of a Christian leader

Please read Titus 1:5-9

The story goes that there was once a light aircraft carrying four people. These were the pilot, two teenage lads and an old Christian man. They were flying along when suddenly the pilot's voice crackled over the intercom: 'We've got serious engine trouble, we're going to crash and there are only three parachutes. I have a wife and a family who need me, so I'm taking one of the parachutes. Goodbye!' And he jumped out leaving the two lads and the old Christian. Immediately one of the teenagers said, 'Actually I have to tell you that I am the brightest, most clever young man in the world. I have an IQ of 175 and the world needs me. I am already a great scientist and I may well invent the cure for cancer or for AIDS. So I'm taking a parachute. Goodbye!' And he jumped out.

At this point the old Christian began to talk to the remaining youngster. He said, 'You take the last parachute. I'm old. I've enjoyed my life and I know that when I die I'm going to be with the Lord Jesus, my Saviour. So you take the last parachute. It's OK.' To which the youngster replied, 'Don't worry. There's no need for that. There are still two parachutes. The brightest boy in the world jumped out with my haversack!'

It is a humorous story which warns us against being overconfident know-it-alls. It reminds us that we need humility and to be teachable. But who is going to teach us? We have

already seen that to learn and receive the truth about the Lord
Jesus Christ is absolutely vital, for by it we gain eternal life.
But who should be our teachers?

It is that question with which this section of Titus is
concerned: **'The reason I left you in Crete was that you
might straighten out what was left unfinished and appoint
elders in every town, as I directed you'** (1:5).

Churches had been started in the towns on the island of
Crete but they were not in good shape. They needed leaders
who would **'hold firmly to the trustworthy message as it has
been taught, so that [they] can encourage others by sound
doctrine and refute those who oppose it'** (1:9). This was
required in every town, in all the churches.

The problem on Crete was what we have called the problem
of the gap. It is the gap between what Christians say they
believe and how they actually behave.

In the last chapter we saw how Paul defined Christian faith.
He called it 'the knowledge of the truth that leads to godliness'
(1:1). But on Crete, something was wrong; the truth was not
leading to godliness as it should.

There is a story from Calcutta we can learn from. A six-
year-old orphan boy had been rescued by Christian aid-
workers from the streets of the city where he had been dying
of fever. They had nursed him back to health and on the day he
was leaving for another home they gave him a packet of sugar.
Sugar is highly prized among the poor there. A quarter of sugar
is equivalent to a day's wages. As the little boy walked out of
the gates he saw the workers carrying in another child, obviously in terrible need. He walked straight over and handed the
sugar to the boy.

'Why have you done that?' he was asked. 'I think that it is
what Jesus would have done,' he replied.

Among the Cretan Christians that kind of thing was not
happening. Though Christ is all generosity, though the gospel

is a message of forgiveness and eternal life freely given to everyone who will receive it, without qualification, yet it had not worked out practically in their lives. They were still caught up in the subjective selfishness of the non-Christian society which surrounded them. They were not filled with the holy, self-sacrificial love of Christ. They were still imprisoned in the sensualism and materialism of a pagan culture very similar to our own. The churches were in that sense self-centred. They were crooked and ingrown, and needed straightening out. How? Where people are self-centred and self-important often there is rivalry and disorganization as people vie with each other. Order needed to be established out of the chaos. How?

Paul's answer is that of appointing Christian leaders for every church. These men (for that is what Paul assumes them to be) are to be men who not only know and teach the truth, but who live it out in their own lives, as examples to others. For Paul church leadership was a vital area. The quality of a church is very often a reflection of the calibre of its leadership. Many of the ills of the churches can be cured by having the right people in leadership.

Blameless leaders

If we survey briefly verses 5-9 a number of general factors concerning church leadership can first be noted.

Paul sums up the work of Christian leadership. He calls them **'elders'** (1:5). This is a term with a Jewish Old Testament background, where it was used to refer to the men of good reputation and wisdom who watched over the affairs of a town or village (Prov. 31:23). This idea was being transferred to the churches. Each church is a community of God's people. The term 'elder' implies that these men should be experienced Christians, with a real measure of maturity in the faith. (Sadly

this does not always go with years.) They were to be men who
could be respected, and able to lead by example and wise
counsel.

Paul also calls them **'overseer[s]'** (1:7). They are men
entrusted to watch over God's work, his church. The idea
behind the use of 'overseer' is twofold. It refers to shepherds,
keeping watch over their flocks, to keep them safe from
wolves or other dangers. It also refers to stewards in a great
house who are seeing that all the servants are doing their work,
and pulling their weight for the master as they should. Elders
are called both to care for the church and to stir up the church
in its work for God.

The Christian leader's tool-kit in undertaking this work is
apostolic truth, by which he can 'encourage ... by sound
doctrine' and 'refute those who oppose it'. For us the Scriptures provide both food for the soul and the sword of the Spirit
for our warfare.

Notice too that Paul directs Titus to appoint elders (plural)
in every town. In the New Testament you will never find
reference to the appointment of 'a pastor' or 'a minister'. The
work of Christian leadership is to be a shared work. The church
is to be led, not by one man, but by a group of men sharing the
leadership. This has many advantages. No man is omni-
competent; he needs others alongside him with other gifts.
When one man is tired and worn out, there are other leaders to
continue to carry the load. Troubles in churches rarely come
one at a time, and more than one person is often needed to help.
A shared leadership also guards against any one man becoming too prominent in a congregation and so obscuring the
headship of Christ over his church.

But as Paul describes the kind of men he looks for in
leadership one word is repeated. It is the word **'blameless'**
(1:6,7). Immoral or unworthy men in Christian leadership are
a shame to Christ's cause. A church leader must be someone

with the highest moral and spiritual standards. He must be a person to whom, since his conversion, no mud sticks. One thinks of the prophet Samuel in his farewell speech asking the people, 'Here I stand. Testify against me in the presence of the Lord… Whom have I cheated? … From whose hand have I accepted a bribe…?' (1 Sam. 12:3). No one could accuse him. With this general qualification of blamelessness in mind, Paul takes time in this paragraph to explain explicitly what he means. Before a man is to be appointed to Christian leadership Paul commands Titus and the churches to examine three specific areas. They must test his <u>family life</u>, <u>his personal</u> <u>conduct</u> and his <u>doctrinal stance</u>.

Family life (1:5-6)

It is interesting that both here and in 1 Timothy 3, where Paul also describes the qualifications required for elders, he starts with the matter of family life. The reason for this is that Paul sees the church and the family as very closely related and intertwined. There is a sense in which the church is God's family. Paul has already referred to Titus as his 'true son in our common faith' (1:4). Very often Christians refer to one another as 'brothers and sisters' in the Lord, and this has biblical precedent (Rom. 16:1,17).

As the church is a family, the way a man brings up and leads his own family is, as it were, a test-bed for how he will get on in leading and nurturing the church. Paul spells this out in 1 Timothy 3:5: 'If anyone does not know how to manage his own family, how can he take care of God's church?' And with equal certainty we can say that if a man has made a good job of his family life, this is a solid basis for believing that he may well be capable of doing a good job for the Lord's family, the local church.

It is because the church and the family are so closely related
that although the New Testament contains a lot of flexibility
in the roles of men and women in the church, it insists that just
as there is to be male headship in the family (Eph. 5:23), so in
the church the buck must stop with a male leadership. The
family and the church are to have the same pattern. Without
this there would be confusion in relationships between men
and women. If a wife were to be in authority over her husband
in the church because she is a church leader, what would
happen to the husband's authority in the home? Whatever we
make of the details of Paul's commands with regard to the
roles of male and female in church, in 1 Corinthians 11 and 14,
or 1 Timothy 2, his great concern is always to maintain the
continuity between the pattern of the family and the pattern of
the church. With this close relationship between home and
church, a man's domestic life gives a good first indication of
whether or not he is gifted for church leadership.

**'An elder must be blameless, the husband of but one
wife, a man whose children believe and are not open to the
charge of being wild and disobedient'** (1:6). The nub of this
verse is that through his family life an elder must be seen to be
someone who is both faithful himself and inspires faithfulness
in others. The church leader is to be a faithful husband to his
wife. Adultery is the shame of the modern church. Paul says
that an elder, even in a culture where monogamy may not be
popular, must be a one-woman man. If he has a faithful heart
for his wife, he will be the kind of man who has a faithful heart
for the local church.

Again, he is to be the kind of man who inculcates faithfulness in his children. The NIV gives a translation of verse 6
which indicates that eldership should be restricted to men
whose whole family, including their children, are believers.
Although such a situation is highly desirable it is probably
going beyond what Paul actually meant. The word 'believe'
can equally be translated 'faithful' or 'trustworthy'. There are

two reasons for suspecting the interpretation which requires the elders' children to be believers. First, his requirement goes beyond what Paul requires of an elder's family in 1 Timothy 3:4: 'He must manage his own family well and see that his children obey him with proper respect.' Secondly, the interpretation 'trustworthy' or 'faithful', in the sense of obedient, makes a more viable contrast with the end of verse 6. They are to be faithful and obedient to their father 'and not open to the charge of being wild and disobedient'.

We have begun to explore the idea that one of the main reasons for the gap between belief and behaviour in Christians today is the prevalence of subjectivism. Psychologists tell us that often a major reason for an anxious preoccupation with self goes back to the way children are being brought up in the late twentieth century. Preoccupation with self almost always leads to some kind of rebellion in a child.

The topic of parenting is vast. We cannot go into great detail here. But, simply speaking, there are two opposites which make for bad parenting. One is neglect of a child. This may be physical or emotional neglect. This leaves a child frustrated. He yearns for love but his parents are never there for him. She looks forward to having Mum and Dad to herself for a while, but they have no time for such silly things, and she is made to feel unimportant and worthless. This leads to resentment and anger in a child and eventually that will boil over into rebellion.

The other extreme of bad parenting is to over-indulge the child. Some parents, because their own husband-wife relationship is not good, place the child in the centre of the family. The welfare of the child is something they can agree on! But this can lead to the parents being willing to do absolutely anything the child desires. The child then (perhaps subconsciously) is able to manipulate his parents and eventually becomes frightened of his own power, not having the maturity to handle it. It is as if the parents have handed responsibility to the child.

Although the child may initially enjoy this power he is actually too young to cope with it, and so begins to resent what his parents are doing in failing to set limits and give guidance to him. Here again is a recipe for an angry, self-centred, exasperated child who will rebel.

If this has happened in a man's family, this same kind of pattern could be passed on to the church. If a man is not loving enough to care for his children, he will not have a heart for the church. If he does not have enough firmness to set limits for his children, how will he have the backbone to bring discipline to the church when it is required?

'No,' says Paul, 'choose a man who gets the right balance of kindness and firmness for his children. He is the kind of man who will have the right balance for the church.'

What about single men as elders? This cannot be excluded. Paul himself was single. But before we appoint single men then some criterion other than married life will have to be found for testing a man's faithfulness and his ability to inspire faithfulness in others. Perhaps a period of work alongside an older leader is required. Of Timothy Paul was able to say, 'You know that Timothy has proved himself, because as a son with his father he has served with me in the work of the gospel' (Phil. 2:22).

Personal conduct (1:7-8)

'Since an overseer is entrusted with God's work, he must be blameless — not overbearing, not quick-tempered, not given to drunkenness, not violent, not pursuing dishonest gain. Rather he must be hospitable, one who loves what is good, who is self-controlled, upright, holy and disciplined.'
A man's personal behaviour patterns form the second test for qualification to Christian leadership.

The literal translation of 'with God's work' in verse 7 is 'as God's steward'. The elder as a steward/overseer calls to mind, as we have previously noted, the image of the local church as God's household. In ancient society a steward of a nobleman's house was charged with responsibility for managing the master's affairs. For such a position integrity, or blameless-ness, was required, as Jesus' parables about a master going away and leaving his property in the charge of stewards indicate. The master will one day return and the steward must be able to give account.

A steward left in such a position has many opportunities to abuse his power. So, a man of absolute personal integrity is required — a man of conscience. Just as personal integrity is required of a steward, so blamelessness must extend to the personal life of a Christian leader, who is God's steward. So Paul now focuses on a prospective elder's personal conduct.

In this section there are, firstly, five things forbidden: **'... not overbearing, not quick-tempered, not given to drunk-enness, not violent, not pursuing dishonest gain'**.

An *overbearing* man is someone who is self-willed and egotistical. A man like this will not be able to listen to the needs of others, and his dominance will cloud the prominence of Christ which should characterize the church. Such a man, though applauded by the world as a strong leader, is not for leadership in the church, where true leadership is humble service (Mark 10:42-45).

A *quick-tempered,* angry man is unfit to work in a team of leaders. Proverbs warns us that an explosive temper very often rubs off on others. Imagine what would happen in the leader-ship team meeting! 'A hot-tempered man stirs up dissension, but a patient man calms a quarrel' (Prov. 15:18). A man with a short fuse will soon explode God's work if he is in leadership.

Next Paul warns against *drunkenness*. Wine was often more a part of everyday mealtimes in the ancient world of the

Mediterranean than perhaps we tea-drinking Britishers are normally used to. This meant that the temptation to drunkenness was much more open. But a drunken shepherd cannot keep watch over his master's sheep. The wolf would have wreaked havoc before the shepherd had even realized what was going on. Just so, an elder must be a person who can control his appetites rather than letting his appetites control him.

Paul warns against *violent* men becoming elders. When our Lord Jesus did not retaliate even when falsely accused and wrongly provoked, and when he has given us a new command to love one another, violence has no place in the Christian church. True spiritual authority is nothing to do with a clenched first and white knuckles.

Lastly in this list of characteristics which rule a man out of Christian leadership, Paul tells us that the elder must not be someone who *pursues dishonest gain.* The Roman poet Livy said, 'The Cretans are as eager for riches as bees for honey.' Such a man will be a man able to be bribed. A lover of money will be willing to say anything for personal gain. He is not a man of integrity. He will not make a faithful steward for God's church, which is built up by truth and love. The love of money characterizes false teachers (1:11). They are happy to teach whatever will make them popular and bring in the cash.

By contrast, Paul now goes on to describe positively blameless personal conduct. In this second section there are six things commanded: **'Rather he must be hospitable, one who loves what is good, who is self-controlled, upright, holy and disciplined.'**

Hospitality, when properly offered, shows a generous heart. It is this kind of spirit Paul is looking for in an elder. Hospitality is not simply about asking your friends round. In particular in Scripture it extends to strangers and outcasts. It is less to do with a loaded table and more to do with an open door for those in physical, mental, emotional or spiritual need (Matt. 25:35).

As we have indicated, the central problem in the Cretan churches was that faith was not leading to goodness in people's lives. The gap was yawning. Against that background Paul emphasizes that elders must be people who lead by example in closing the gap. He must be *'one who loves what is good'*. A Christian leader needs to be one devoted to promoting wholesome humanity and gracious godliness, even if other people do deride him as 'squeaky clean'.

The word *'self-controlled'* which Paul uses here can just as well be translated 'sensible'. An elder must not be a man given to wild, foolish ideas. Yes, he must be a man who believes that God is the God of the impossible. But he must mix such a faith with a good dose of common sense. The God who gave us our hearts is also the same God who gave us our heads!

The remaining three qualities, 'upright, holy and disciplined', complete the profile of the blameless personal life required in one who aspires to Christian leadership. *Uprightness* refers to straightness in our relations with other people. *Holiness* refers to dedication in our relationship to God. *Discipline* speaks of a man's relations to himself. He must be one in full control of his own appetites, actions, moods and aspirations.

Here, then, we have a well-rounded picture of the kind of man the church needs for its leadership. What I fear is that such men are out of fashion. Such men are of little account in many people's minds today. The secular world, with its blaring egotism and slavery to novelty, despises such men as boring. And the modern church, which similarly views everything through the tinted glasses of subjectivism, sets little store by such men. Christians whose first unspoken question is to ask, 'How does he make me feel?' are ill-fitted to appreciate the qualities required. They put more store by a man's entertainment value than his faithfulness. They are more concerned with the gifts of the Spirit than the fruit of the Spirit.

No, when we come to think about who should lead the church, and who should teach us, ~~do not ask, 'Is he amusing?'~~, ~~or 'Is he attractive to look at?'~~, or 'How many people come to listen to him?', or even 'Has he a great intellect?' These questions are at best secondary and at worst ultimately utterly irrelevant. The questions which must be asked and answered plainly are to do with a man's moral and spiritual quality. He must match up to Paul's test of being blameless.

Blameless men are out of fashion. But nevertheless the apostle tells us that it is such men, and only such men, who are to lead God's church.

Gospel stance (1:9)

Last, but by no means least, Paul commands that the doctrinal convictions of a man under consideration for leadership in the church must be investigated: **'He must hold firmly to the trustworthy message as it has been taught, so that he can encourage others by sound doctrine and refute those who oppose it.'**

We are told two things here about the Christian leader and the apostolic message. We are told how he must hold it, and how he must use it.

1. How he is to hold the message

Firstly, he must hold it *firmly*. There always have been, and always will be, pressures on the Christian leader to let the gospel, the message of Scripture, slip. It is tragic to see the effects on the church down the centuries when for various reasons the church and its gospel have drifted apart.

Paul emphasizes two aspects of the Bible's message. First he emphasizes its *trustworthiness*. It is a trustworthy message which church leaders are called to hold to firmly. Paul himself was an eyewitness of the resurrection of the Lord Jesus Christ. In that most dramatic meeting on the Damascus road his life had been turned around completely from a persecutor of Christ to a preacher of Christ. The apostle, as he writes to Titus, is a living evidence of the truth of the gospel. Today the pressure to let go of 'the holy Scriptures, which are able to make you wise for salvation through faith in Christ Jesus' is enormous and comes from many different directions. In particular, our day pursues the philosophy of pluralism. This is the idea that all religions are equally true. And of course, the implication is that if all religions are equally true we should not be so concerned to hold firmly to the scriptural message.

G. E. Lessing, the eighteenth-century German dramatist and critic, argued for pluralism with a story. He said a father had a magic ring which he was duty-bound to bequeath to one of his three sons when he died. Not wanting to be accused of favouritism, he made two imitation rings. Before his death he gave each of his sons a ring. Each one thought his was the real one and an argument broke out between them as to who was the owner of the genuine ring. The three sons went to Nathan the wise. He told them, 'Let each think his own is the true one, but do not try to persuade anyone else.' 'No one can be sure which religion is true, so don't push your own on others and do not be too worried about truth,' is the moral of the story.

But a faithful Christian leader will not swallow that. God does not lie, as Paul has told us in verse 2. He does not make imitation rings. He has given his Son and the one true gospel to the whole world, as is evidenced not least by the resurrection of Jesus and the godliness which the gospel is capable of producing in people's lives. The elder must be a man who holds to the trustworthy message and will not let the church be robbed of it by flattering words or fashionable arguments. It is such men who are to be our teachers, and no others.

Secondly, Paul underlines the *carefulness* with which Christian leaders must handle the gospel they hold on to. They must hold on to the message **'as it has been taught'**. Here is an indicator of another point of attack on the gospel to which we need to pay attention. Many critics come against the apostolic gospel by saying, 'Yes, the New Testament was the message of the apostles to the ancient world, but now the world is so different. We live in a very different age, an age of technology and where we have understood far more about psychology, genetics and why people do as they do. The gospel needs to change with the times. All this talk of sin is not helpful. Talk of the wrath of a holy God is off-putting to people. The gospel needs to be updated.'

But the faithful Christian leader sees through all that. He holds to the gospel 'as it has been taught' by Paul and by the Lord Jesus. Of course, we need to use modern language in communicating the gospel. Of course, we need to apply the gospel to the situations and needs of a modern technological society. But we do not change the message. Why? Because although times change, God is still the same; fallen human nature is still the same; the Lord Jesus is the same yesterday, today and for ever; man's need of eternal salvation is the same; and the grace and generosity of God are still the same. So the men to teach the church must be men who hold on to the gospel 'as it has been taught'.

This is the vital truth. In Paul's view, to change the gospel is to be worthy of being cursed (Gal. 1:8-9). If only the truth can save the lost, then to neglect it or tamper with it, simply in order to gain popularity, or to be thought more respectable, is to be guilty of the most heinous crime against humanity.

The faithful leader, then, is not someone who toys with, or is hazy about, the central truths of Christianity. He must be one who teaches the gospel clearly and without compromise.

2. *How he is to use the message*

But not only does Paul tell us how such a leader must hold on to the biblical message, he also tells us how the man must use that message. He holds on to the Bible's message **'so that he can encourage others by sound doctrine and refute those who oppose it'**. His ministry is twofold. There is encouragement and refutation; building up the church, and knocking down error.

The gospel is a great message of *encouragement* to fallen sinners. It is the message of the 'kindness and love of God' (3:4). As Christians live in a fallen world, struggling with the corruption and weakness within themselves, and the wiles of the devil attacking from outside, they are often in need of encouragement. The gospel is the message that gives us hope, and puts heart into us to continue.

Paul here speaks of 'sound' doctrine. That word 'sound' is a word doctors sometimes use. The old physicians used to speak of being 'sound of wind and limb', and when they used that expression they meant that someone was healthy. Teaching of the true gospel will produce spiritually healthy Christians. As it is properly received, the truth will lead to godliness, whereas error will lead to spiritually sick Christians. The phrase 'sound doctrine' is scorned in many Christian circles, sadly, but actually it is one of the church's greatest needs in order for Christians to be holy and happy in the Lord. The pure gospel is the source of the Christian's joy.

Commenting on the ministry of George Whitefield, the eighteenth-century evangelist, J. C. Ryle remarks, 'He was a man of a singularly happy and cheerful spirit. No one who saw him could ever doubt he enjoyed his religion... A venerable lady of New York, after his death, when speaking of the influences by which the Spirit won her heart to God, used these remarkable words, "Mr Whitefield was so cheerful that it tempted me to become a Christian!"' Any faithful leader must similarly be someone who by his teaching is able to encourage others with the gospel.

But here is a second aspect to the true teacher's work. His sword must be double-edged. Not only must he use Scripture to cut down the sinner's fears, and sever the bonds of darkness, he must also be able to *slay sin and false teaching*. He must be able to 'refute those who oppose' the gospel. This is not such a popular work as the ministry of encouragement. It often has to be a grim battle which requires courage. It is hard for the teacher, for Christians would often far rather be cheered than warned. Combating dangerous error is often caricatured as 'judgementalism' and 'just being negative'. Well, the teacher does need to beware not to fall into an overcritical spirit. But the job of defending the truth and contending for the faith once for all entrusted to the saints is of utmost importance, because it is the truth which alone sets people free and leads to salvation. The true Christian leader has therefore to be a watchman. He must be alive to the philosophies of the modern world and to the cults and to the errors that spring up within the churches, and be able to refute them. It is said that to train people to spot counterfeit banknotes, the best preparation is to set them counting the genuine notes. Thus they become so familiar with the genuine that they can readily spot anything false. Just so, the best preparation for refuting error is a thorough and deep grasp of the Bible and the genuine gospel it teaches.

Can you see why all this is so important? God offers eternal life to the world in Jesus Christ. That eternal life comes to us as we hear and respond to the truth about Christ. That truth is therefore precious. It needs to be taught, passed on across the world, and down the generations. But there are so many false ideas around. How can we tell who is a true teacher and who is a deceiver? Whom should we listen to?

Paul has given us the answer. You can tell a true Christian leader from a false teacher as you investigate his family life, his personal conduct and his gospel stance. As you look at these areas, you will see that although the man may not be perfect, there is a real Christlikeness about him. In the true teacher's life, the truth has already led to godliness, and that is the reason you can trust him to teach you.

3.
False teachers and their followers

Please read Titus 1:9-16

As we have seen, a very important part of the Christian leader's task is to oppose false teaching (1:9). So this section of the letter to Titus follows on closely from the previous paragraph. Having spelt out something of what is required in the life and character of a church leader, Paul goes on now to talk about the false teachers who were troubling the churches in Crete and the people who were following them.

National characteristics

The problems on Crete were complex. As we read this paragraph we realize that false teaching was in a way only half the problem. The Cretan people were particularly vulnerable to liars. The errors of the false teachers seemed to be finding success because they somehow seemed to match what we might call the national character of the Cretans. Together these two formed a very potent and spiritually dangerous cocktail.

We make jokes about English reserve, Scottish prudence, Welsh sentimentality and Irish simplicity. All this is usually not malicious, but good-humoured banter. But they are examples of national characteristics or regional stereotypes. They are generalizations about people from different backgrounds.

They can be hurtful, because generalizations are never accurate and insensitive remarks about race and background can understandably upset people. Yet sometimes there is enough truth in such generalizations to keep the ideas alive. We speak of the Germans' discipline, of Chinese being inscrutable, of the fiery Latin temperament.

Here, in verse 12, Paul refers to the national character of the Cretans. He is quoting a poet from the sixth century B.C. named Epimenides, who was himself from Crete (so he should know!): **'Even one of their own prophets has said, "Cretans are always liars, evil brutes, lazy gluttons."'**

This letter to Titus has already shown us that the gospel of the Lord Jesus Christ is 'the truth that leads to godliness' (1:1). But the problem on Crete was that this was not happening. There was a gap between their Christian life and their behaviour. The truth was not leading to godliness. Their lives were self-centred and out of step with God's love.

The first major factor in hindering the churches on the path to godliness was false teaching. **'There are many rebellious people, mere talkers and deceivers ... teaching things they ought not to teach'** (1:10-11). But also the national predilections of the Cretans played a part. In their self-centredness and sensualism, the Cretans were particularly open to both teaching and receiving false ideas into their lives.

Where do national characteristics originate? We have to say, first of all, that all mankind, from whatever background, are sinners and inherit that basic self-centred nature from the Fall in the Garden of Eden. So when we speak of national characteristics we are definitely not saying that one nation or one race is intrinsically better or worse than another. What we are doing is simply asking how our common sinfulness expresses itself in different people in the light of different backgrounds. Concerning the Cretan mentality and its connection with false teaching there are two points to make.

Firstly, we may speculate that geography, trade and climate had some influence on them. Where the climate is warm and food abundant, people do tend to be more relaxed. Where life is colder and harder, national characteristics tend to be those of hard work and discipline. Perhaps the former tend to the sins of self-indulgence while the latter tend to the sins of self-righteousness. However it came about, Paul identifies the Cretans as generally self-indulgent, wanton and sensual people: 'evil brutes', 'lazy gluttons'. The bodily instincts were primary.

Strangely, such an attitude to life always makes people susceptible to false religious teaching. We know that the five physical senses are sources of pleasure, but they can never ultimately satisfy a person. Carnal gratification does not last for long. 'The eye never has enough of seeing, nor the ear its fill of hearing,' says the writer of Ecclesiastes. So the sensual person is always someone on the lookout for something new, something unusual, something novel. And when a new spiritual teaching which promises ultimate fulfilment, excitement, or a good time comes along such folk are often very open to it. This is a fertile field for false teachers with novel religious teachings which promise special knowledge, or experiences, or prosperity and a 'victorious life of abundance'.

In our modern world, society is set up for just the same thing. The prevalent theory of evolution insists that people are just complicated animals. The implication is that ultimately pleasure lies in the five bodily senses, so wherever we itch we must scratch. But such gratification leaves people unfulfilled, and therefore vulnerable to any kind of religious teaching which panders to the basic self-centred, pleasure-oriented view of life.

But coming back to the character of the Cretans, we must realize that, secondly, national characteristics are bound up greatly with prevalent ideas and the significant moments in the history of the nation. We speak of the 'Dunkirk spirit' of the

British, for example. Cretans historically had acquired a name
for being liars. This, it seems, had arisen because back in time,
they had claimed that the tomb of Zeus, the lord of the gods,
was on Crete. This lie had probably brought attention and
traffic to the island. A lie had helped them. This had set a
significant precedent in the national mindset. The idea of
peddling religious ideas for gain, regardless of whether they
were true or false, was something which had become a
perfectly acceptable way of carrying on. And of course a false
teacher is only too happy to trim his teachings to suit what
people want to hear.

The false teachers of Crete of Paul's day were simply
following in the footsteps of a well-worn tradition: 'Cretans
are always liars.' They fulfilled the 'prophecy' of Epimenides
in their own generation by propagating a religious lie.

Here, then, on the island of Crete was a deadly chemistry
which was resistant to the progress of the gospel: error and a
readiness to accept.

How are Christian leaders to deal with this dual problem of
false teaching and a national predeliction to it? That is Paul's
agenda in this section. Because it is so closely linked to the
previous paragraph concerning the qualities required in
elders, we will back up a little and take in from verse 9 down
to verse 16. Paul's answer to the problem is to confront people
and their error with the truth. Truth is always Christianity's
great weapon. We can divide the section in four parts. Paul
gives three steps for dealing with the false teachers and then he
explains why this must be done.

They must be refuted (1:9-10)

The elder must **'hold firmly to the trustworthy message ...
and refute those who oppose it. For there are many**

rebellious people, mere talkers and deceivers, especially those of the circumcision group.'

Perhaps you have come across the children's picture-book game *Where's Wally?* In the US he is called Waldo. This lanky character Wally has a cheerful face and red-and-white bobble hat and the game is to find him in the picture. The problem is that he is hidden amidst an enormous crowd of other characters. Different pictures have him in the crowds on the beach or at the back of the fairground etc. In many ways that, according to verse 10, sums up one of the devil's most potent tactics against the gospel. He knows people need to hear and grasp the truth of the Lord Jesus Christ in order that they might find eternal life, so his ploy is to surround the gospel with a tremendous crowd of spurious alternatives. It makes it hard to find the truth.

'There are many rebellious people, mere talkers and deceivers,' says Paul. Satan floods the market with decoys. Paul describes the false teachers and their adherents as *rebellious* people. They do not promote a spirit of submission to God and to his Word. Very often their message is more to do with self-fulfilment than submission. And if their teaching does include submission it is frequently to do with submission to cult leaders rather than to Christ and the Bible. But the true gospel does bring a willing acquiescence and commitment to the Lord. 'Take my yoke upon you and learn from me,' said Jesus.

Paul describes these opponents of the gospel as *mere talkers*. These people talk a lot, but they say nothing of any lasting worth. Their teaching is all theory, but shows little or nothing by way of leading people to practical godly living in the daily round.

Paul describes the false teachers as *deceivers*. They peddle in false promises. Their teaching is not the gospel given by the God 'who does not lie' (1:2). What they have to offer leads nowhere but to destruction. In recent years we have seen the tragedies perpetrated by the Branch Davidians at Waco,

Texas, and the gas attack on innocent people by the Japanese Oum Sect on the Tokyo underground. After the mass killings in Switzerland associated with the so-called Order of the Solar Temple, a spokesman in that country said that he feared there were as many as 600 different cults in Switzerland. It should not surprise us. Paul said there are many deceivers. And sometimes, as with the Jonestown mass suicides in Guyana in the 1970s, these cultish movements can begin within a fairly orthodox Christian background, where people are deceived.

But we would be foolish to focus simply on the more extreme cults. There are many other opponents of the gospel with a far more credible and respectable pedigree. Paul's own ministry had suffered most from Jewish opposition, from those whom Paul described as having a zeal for God but not based on knowledge (Rom. 10:2). Many of his own missionary activities had been assailed by his Jewish fellow-countrymen. In many ways the religion of the Jews, based as it is in God's Old Testament revelation, is a great religion. But in their rejection of Jesus, God's Messiah, and their continuing to cling to the Old Testament rituals which God had done away with in Christ, Paul has to include 'the circumcision group' among the rebellious and deceivers.

What does Paul say must be our response? Where does the church begin in dealing with false teaching? Paul says that it must be refuted (1:9). That is the only place to start. All Christians have some responsibility here, but it is particularly the work of elders and church leaders. Research must be carried out thoroughly into what the error is which is being taught. We must get our facts straight. Then the ideas of the heretics must be analysed and exposed and shown to be false. In order to do that, our tool is 'the trustworthy message' (1:9) of the biblical, apostolic gospel. False teaching is to be out-argued from the plain teaching of Scripture. The Bible is our great weapon. This was Paul's great weapon too. Of his ministry in Thessalonica we read, 'As his custom was, Paul went into the synagogue and ... he reasoned with them from the Scriptures, explaining and proving that Christ had to suffer and rise from the dead' (Acts 17:2-3). The Old Testament prophecies in particular, written hundreds of years in advance, and fulfilled in Christ before many eyewitnesses, provide a massive argument for the truth of the gospel.

False teaching is not dealt with by ignoring it. It is certainly not to be dealt with in terms of physical force, as with the Catholic Spanish Inquisition. Neither is it best handled by a pooling of ideas in a multi-faith discussion. Paul tells us that false teaching is to be disproved by reasoned argument. It is to be refuted.

This is an important point. There is a market-place of beliefs. We ourselves live in a multi-cultural, religiously pluralistic society. But Paul's assumption here is that we live in a logical world. In God's providence we have been given the light of reason. The laws of logic are transcultural. They apply just as much to a Hindu as to a Christian. They apply just as much to the heretic as to the orthodox. And therefore, though it might be hard work, with Bible in hand, we are to use our minds and our reasoning to refute what is false. For if the gospel is the true message of salvation, from God our Creator, then it will match reality and prove valid under every legitimate test of truth.

They must be silenced (1:11-13)

'They must be silenced, because they are ruining whole households by teaching things they ought not to teach — and that for the sake of dishonest gain.' What Paul means here is that false teachers must be so shown to be wrong that no one will want to listen to them. Their error must be demonstrated so clearly that if it is felt necessary to place them under church discipline for their heresy, it will be plain to everyone that such action is just. Perhaps when all their ideas have been exhausted, as shown to be wrong, they will either give up and go away, or, better still, repent and give themselves to the true gospel. Either way they must be silenced.

This is necessary, says Paul, because ideas do influence people. If the false teaching is allowed to carry on it will subvert people away from Christ and into lifestyles which are neither good for them nor glorifying to God. Paul speaks of the heretics on Crete 'ruining whole households by teaching things they ought not to teach'. Here 'households' could refer to churches meeting in houses, or to Christian families. Religious ideas which pander to a self-centred generation, promising personal fulfilment and freedom, will not want to know about responsibilities and things which might restrict personal freedom, like family duties. It is not just that groups were believing false doctrines. False doctrines always have an effect on how we live.

From Paul's teaching in chapter 2 of Titus it seems that the effect of the false doctrine was to undermine the conduct of family life, and male and female roles within the family (cf. 2:1-4). Where God's pattern for family living is undermined it always brings hurt and heartache. The false teachers peddled lies. As we have already seen, Paul quotes Epimenides: 'Even one of their own prophets has said, "Cretans are always liars, evil brutes, lazy gluttons." This testimony is true.' Where husbands are not taught the pure doctrine of Christ they will have no incentive to love their wives as Christ loved the church. Often they become 'evil brutes, lazy gluttons', to the detriment of everyone else in the family. Where wives are not taught to respect their husbands out of love for Christ, they too can degenerate. In chapter 2 Paul warns against women becoming slanderers, drinkers or lazy. All this can lead to hurt children and to the breakdown of family life. And it all flows out of wrong ideas, false teaching, be it religious or secular, being imbibed by people. Therefore false teaching must be silenced.

It was not even as if the false teachers had sincere motives in their ministry. They were actually not the kind of people who genuinely had the good of their hearers at heart, but were misguided. Their real motive in teaching, says Paul, is 'for the sake of dishonest gain'. The preacher's fees and expenses were uppermost in their minds. This again was the natural Cretan way. It is a warning to us all to regard with suspicion any religious meeting where the collection plate is too prominent. With such a motivation behind that teaching, Paul is telling us, it will be no loss to the world if such teachers no longer teach.

They must be rebuked (1:13-14)

'Therefore, rebuke them sharply, so that they will be sound in the faith and will pay no attention to Jewish myths or to the commands of those who reject the truth.' Not only must the false teachers be refuted and silenced, but they and their followers should be rebuked. They must be corrected with verbal force. Heresy is a serious and damaging matter and it cannot be addressed lightly. People need to see that Christian leaders are earnest. Note Paul's use of the adverb 'sharply'. These people need to be told in no uncertain terms that they have been wrong to follow such error. Paul's concern here is not to be vicious, but to lead them to proper repentance and to set them back on track walking with the Lord! They need to be rebuked 'so that they will be sound in the faith'. False teachers and their adherents can be rescued from fatal error!

Before his conversion to Christ, the sixteenth-century Reformer Hugh Latimer was a ferocious proponent of Roman Catholicism. He would literally scare people away from listening to evangelical expositions of Scripture. But despite his fearful reputation, a young student, Thomas Bilney, asked for a private interview with Latimer, and there clearly confessed his faith in Christ. The result was that Latimer was converted. Those who promote error can be turned round. That is Paul's desire.

His seeming sternness comes from a heart of love. The certain Word of God has been replaced by weird and wonderful 'myths' and stories. The Word of God, which will never pass away, has been replaced in the minds of people by 'the commands of those who reject the truth', who are not only here today and gone tomorrow, but by rejecting the truth have already proved themselves to be blind guides. If people are going to be disabused of such dangerous ideas, then it will take a certain amount of forcefulness.

Today's church leaders often lack that proper sternness which is sometimes required. A balance must be struck, but often the pastor is too concerned to be charming rather than to be helpful. Calvin, in his *Institutes of the Christian Religion,* speaks of the authority of leaders to do such things in the Word of God: 'Here is the supreme power with which pastors of the church, by whatever name they are called, should be invested — namely to dare all boldly for the word of God; counselling all virtue, glory, wisdom and rank of the world to yield to obey its majesty; to command all from the highest to the lowest, trusting to its power to build up the house of Christ and overthrow the house of Satan; to feed the sheep and chase away the wolves; to instruct and exhort the docile, to accuse, rebuke and subdue the rebellious and petulant, to bind and loose; in time, if need be, to file and fulminate, but all in the word of God' (*Institutes,* 4.8.9).

With what we have seen in mind, it is as well to pause a moment and collect together in our minds a picture of the false teacher. If earlier in the chapter we have seen the marks of a true Christian leader, so that we shall know whom to choose to teach us, it is as well to gain an idea of the marks of false teachers, in order to know whom to avoid. There are four marks which suggest themselves from this passage:

1. False teachers *reject or subvert the plain teaching of Scripture* (1:10), trying to subtly explain it away and replace the authority of Scripture with something else.

2. False teachers *lead people into ungodliness* (1:11). Their adherents are either led into sins of decadence, flouting God's law, or into sins of self-righteousness, flouting God's love. Either way they pander to people's self-centredness (1:12).

3. False teachers are very often *motivated by gaining money* (1:11) and invent all kinds of ploys to induce you to give it to them. We do need to give our money. But isn't it interesting that both the Lord Jesus and the apostles were always more concerned that people give their money to the poor rather than to them? (Mark 10:21; Gal. 2:10).

4. Lastly, because as we have been emphasizing, it is part of the responsibility of the local church elders and leaders to oppose false teaching, very often false teachers seek to operate outside the structure or control of local churches. False teachers love to have special meetings.

But, praise the Lord, false teachers and their followers can be rescued from the error of their ways. Note Paul's progression. They must be refuted, silenced and lovingly but sharply rebuked!

Now, all this does not sit too well with the ethos of today's Christianity, nor with the general outlook of the world at the end of the twentieth century. 'Paul,' we might say, 'all this looks a little too unloving and narrow. It appears to be somewhat too definite and dogmatic in its approach.' Paul addresses such concern in the last two verses of the chapter.

Paul's defence of dogmatism

Why must we be so straight about the truth of the Lord Jesus Christ? **'To the pure, all things are pure, but to those who are corrupted and do not believe, nothing is pure. In fact, both their minds and consciences are corrupted. They claim to know God, but by their actions they deny him. They are detestable, disobedient and unfit for doing anything good.'** Why be so dogmatic about the gospel? There are two elements to Paul's answer.

1. Cleansing through the gospel

The prevalent false teaching in Crete seems to have been rooted in a Jewish background (1:14). Paul's references to the idea of 'purity' in verse 15 suggest that the heretics were people with a heavy emphasis on what was 'clean' and what was 'unclean' similar to that of the Pharisees of Jesus' day. They were concerned with rites and ceremonies, which included religious washing, and perhaps abstinence from certain foods. Ritual purity was seen as the way to God. This may well have left people free to pursue wayward ethical behaviour in other areas of their lives. 'So long as I have completed the required ceremony I am free to do as I please.' Such an idea would have commended itself to the sensual Cretans.

But Paul knew that real purity in God's sight is neither a matter of rituals, nor indeed of our own good deeds, for even these are as filthy rags in the sight of the all-holy God (Isa. 64:6). True purity in God's sight is something which God alone can bestow upon us, and he does that through Christ alone. To be acceptable to God we must receive Christ by faith. It is never what we do for God that can cleanse us, but what he has done for us in the Lord Jesus. Jesus is the Lamb of God who takes away the sin of the world, by his sacrifice at Calvary. His totally sufficient work for sinners is received personally by faith. So it is that in our verses Paul equates 'those who are corrupted' (that is impure), with being those who 'do not believe' (1:15). Since only Christ can make us accepted in God's sight, nothing that those who do not believe can do can ever make them pure in the sight of God. To them, **'Nothing is pure.'**

However, **'To the pure'** (that is, those who do believe), **'all things are pure.'** What Christ has accomplished for us at Calvary justifies us for ever in God's sight. All our sins are covered. This does not give us licence to sin, but it does mean that we are totally acceptable to God, and nothing can ever undo that. In that sense to us 'all things are pure'. But this blessing is only ours in Christ.

John Bunyan's conversion story is pertinent to us here. The tinker had been brought under conviction and had confessed his sins many times, but he got no peace. But one day, while in an agony over his sins, it was as if he heard the voice of God speaking to his soul. 'Your righteousness is in heaven!' said the voice. He suddenly realized what it meant. His focus of attention suddenly shifted away from himself to Jesus, risen and ascended into heaven and accepted in God's presence. Jesus is accepted in God's presence as the representative for believing sinners. Bunyan suddenly saw that his acceptance with God was not down to him, or his feelings, or even his good or bad behaviour. It was all down to Jesus. Since Jesus was accepted as the sinner's representative, righteous in God's sight in heaven, then so was John Bunyan! Such realization so burst upon Bunyan's understanding that he rejoiced in Christ! It is a wonderful message. There is acceptance with God for even the worst of sinners through Jesus Christ.

Now we see the first part of Paul's defence of dogmatism. Since salvation is only in Jesus, then we must preach only Jesus, for there is no other way. Since he is the only way, it is to do despite to him to preach anything else. False teaching damns people's souls, and so must be opposed. It is only Christ who can cleanse us in God's sight.

2. *The life of the gospel*

At a practical level pure living, according to Jesus, is not about what goes into a person, but what comes out. It is not first of all about keeping rules and regulations; it is about the motives of the heart (Mark 7:17-23). The heart is what Paul speaks of in verse 15 in terms of the mind and the conscience.

Since the Fall every part of our human nature has been affected by sin. Even our consciences have been affected so that we do not recognize the difference between good and evil as we should. With such corrupted consciences people cannot see to discern the truth and therefore to live in the right way. The conscience is that faculty by which, when it is functioning properly, we apprehend the will of God and, as we do what is right, know his approval. But the damaged conscience of sinful man is such that while doing things which are detestable to God, we can think we are doing the right thing.

Further, such is our corruption of mind and conscience that we can deceive ourselves into thinking we are doing right when in fact what we are involved in is evil. **'Both their minds and consciences are corrupted. They claim to know God, but by their actions they deny him.'** Such inward corruption brings forth Paul's remark concerning the false teachers and their followers: **'They are detestable, disobedient and unfit for doing anything good.'**

The conscience can be cleansed only by the blood of Christ (Heb. 9:14). The mind can be transformed, but only by the gospel (Rom. 12:1-2). The heart can be renewed, but only by washing and renewal of the Holy Spirit (3:5). Rules and rituals cannot renew the inward part of people and give them pure motives and godly values. False teaching cannot set people free from their inner bondage to self and sin. Christless religion cannot set people free from their guilt, and doubts and fears. Only the gospel can do these things.

Here, then, is Paul's second reason for being so straight in defence of the truth. Because he loves people, and longs to see them set free from sin and self to serve God with a forgiven rejoicing heart, they must have the gospel and nothing else. It is not a narrow mind, or bigotry, which is the basis for Paul's strident contention for the gospel. His defence of dogmatism is out of a heart of love for people. It is not Paul who has got it wrong. It is the church of today which has got things wrong. To entertain heresy is not enlightened and large-hearted. False teaching is the murderer of souls. It is a dogmatic viewpoint for the biblical truth concerning the gospel of our Lord Jesus Christ which is the most loving stance in the world.

Suppose a hundred people came to a doctor's surgery and he diagnosed them all to have the same illness. Would it be right for him to let them decide which medicine they, in their ignorance, think might be best for them? Would it be narrow-minded of the doctor to recommend that if they all have the same sickness then they all require the same medicine? Of course not.

Life is short,
Death is sure,
Sin the cause
And Christ the cure.

The sickness of the whole world is sin. The one cure for sin is Christ. That is why Paul is a Christian dogmatist.

4.
The pattern of godly manhood

Please read Titus 2:1-8

During World War II my father was sent with the British army to the Far East. In 1941 he was captured by the Japanese when Singapore fell into their hands. The conditions in the prisoner-of-war camps run by the Japanese in those times are illustrated by the fact that of 380 men of my father's company who went into Changi Jail in Singapore my father was one of only twenty-seven who came out alive at the end of the war. The conditions were atrocious and remain infamous.

The situation for allied prisoners in the renowned prison camp on the River Kwai were so abysmal and the death rate so high that the men became almost like animals in their selfishness and desperate struggle to survive. They thought nothing of stealing food or water from dying mates. 'He was going to die anyway,' would be the justification. It was every man for himself.

But in the midst of all this eyewitnesses tell us that a kind of 'miracle' happened. Men began to change. They began to stop stealing and start giving. The selfishness of the struggle for survival gave way to kindness and thoughtfulness for others. It all began with a Scotsman named Angus McGilvray who literally gave his life for his friend. The friend was very ill and about to die. Someone had stolen his blanket; Angus gave him his own. Someone stole the man's food; Angus replaced it with his food ration. The result was that Angus's friend got better, but Angus died. 'Greater love has no one than this,' said Jesus, 'that he lay down his life for his friends' (John 15:13). Angus McGilvray paid the price of greatest love.

This story began to get around the camp. It was the talking point among the prisoners. As the story spread it began to make people think. They were confronted with an example of Christian love. It somehow touched their hearts. And men began to change. Amid the worst possible conditions, where you could be forgiven for thinking that people almost had the right to steal and be selfish, love broke through. Instead of every man for himself, Christian kindness emerged, like a miracle.

Godliness

There is a lifestyle which is never out of date, which is relevant to every culture, which is right whatever the circumstances, for it is eternal life made visible in this world. Paul calls it 'godliness'. What Paul is telling Titus in the first verse of the second chapter of his letter is that this lifestyle flows out of the gospel of the Lord Jesus Christ. This lifestyle of godliness is both the logical consequence and living result of the good news of forgiveness and new life in Christ being accepted into our hearts. It is the healthy living expression of the gospel. He writes to Titus, **'You must teach what is in accord with sound doctrine.'**

What he has in mind is the lifestyle of godliness, as is obvious from the following verses in which he goes on to spell out some of the basic principles of Christian living for men and women. The idea of 'soundness' is to do with health. It is 'sound' teaching which will lead to spiritually and morally healthy Christian lives — the kind of lives Paul goes on to describe. Healthy Christian living is not inevitable for a converted person. The life of God is there in the converted person's heart. There is a motivation to live for God. But Christians need to be guided in how to live. Paul is telling Titus that Christian ethics, the principles of how to conduct our lives, are not something detached from the gospel. Our ethics flow out of the gospel. Christ is not only our Saviour, he is our example. Our approach to life squares with the gospel; it is 'in accord with sound doctrine'.

The false teaching we looked at in the previous chapter which commended itself so much to the naturally unruly Cretan character was a lie. It was based on a very subjective, self-centred outlook on life, which in turn led to ungodly behaviour.

Paul, in verse 11 of chapter 1, spoke of this teaching 'ruining whole households'. The early churches met in houses, and it may be that Paul had in mind that Christian fellowships were being ruined by this teaching. This was no doubt true. But since his emphasis in the opening verses of chapter 2 is centred on domestic life, it is probable that what Paul had in mind was that families, Christian households, were being greatly damaged by this teaching.

Subjectivism does that. If our first, unconscious, controlling thought about anything is 'What about me?' or 'How does this make me feel?' then we are inevitably led to rebel against any kind of restrictions, even the restrictions which arise from family responsibilities. The wrong-headed view of individual freedom which dominates the Western world at the present time has steadily eroded family life. People get divorced because they want to feel 'free'. A self-centred attitude to life encourages us to kick against any limitations, any duty, other than perhaps those for which we get paid.

'Titus, this is ruining people, churches and families,' Paul is saying. 'You have got to spell out to them the lifestyle which is in accord with sound doctrine.' They need teaching about how to live in agreement with the gospel.

What is that gospel lifestyle? What does godliness look like on the practical level? How does it shape the lives of men and women? What does it demand of the youth and the elderly? Paul answers those questions in verses 2-8 of chapter 2. We can summarize what he has to say to everyone in the form of a table.

	Men	Women
Older	Temperate Worthy of respect Self-controlled Sound in faith, love and endurance	Reverent Not slanderers Not addicted to much wine To teach what is good
Younger	Encouraged to be self-controlled	Love husbands and children Self-controlled Pure Busy at home Kind Subject to husbands

In this chapter we shall concentrate on what Paul has to say to the men, and in the next chapter consider his instructions to the women. We shall look at older men, then at younger men.

Older men (2:2)

Paul does not give a definition of what he means by older men, but presumably he is speaking of those who have left their parental home some time ago, who have lived long enough to have had some experience of life and therefore are those to whom others look for advice and example. They may or may not be elderly, but they are mature.

I came across a tongue-in-cheek definition of the male of the human species.[1] It runs like this:

Atomic weight	75 kgs (+ 25 kg)
Occurrences	Wherever there are members of the opposite sex, or large quantities of food and drink.
Physical properties	Very active in early development, with a great affinity for dirt, grime, etc. In time, displays surface fungus and equalization of the horizontal and vertical dimensions. Hard and brittle on the outside when mature, but still soft underneath.
Chemical properties	Turns to jelly when placed alongside stunning sample of female species. Glows brightly when placed in the limelight but becomes invisible when actually needed. Apparently very complex but very easy to analyse as the way to the heart is through the stomach.
Uses	Hardly any.
Caution	Likely to fall to pieces if dropped, rejected, or cut down to size.

It is a humorous and in some ways insightful picture of the modern male. But if it bears any resemblance to the truth, then the modern male is actually a rather pathetic figure, full of beef and bravado superficially, but someone who has never really grown up. On the inside he is easily hurt. It is really a picture of men living behind a mask of tough masculinity (so-called), while on the inside they are vulnerable and lost. I think it is a fair picture. People realize this. Men are often very self-protective. The singer/song-writer Paul Simon has an old song with the lines:

> There's a wall in China,
> It's a thousand miles long,
> And there's a wall around me
> You can't even see.
> It took a little time
> To get next to me.

That is why so many wives feel as if they don't really know their husbands. In our vulnerability we men build walls around ourselves. Men are in need. They may lose their jobs. Relationships may go wrong. But they are not going to cry. They are going to hide under the hard shell of 'masculinity'. Their strength is on the outside; it is in the mask they wear, to protect their inner vulnerability.

How very different is Paul's picture of what a mature Christian man should be! He tells Titus, **'Teach the older men to be temperate, worthy of respect, self-controlled, and sound in faith, in love and in endurance.'**

Paul presents a picture of winsome masculine strength of outward character, which is based on a healthy spiritual life on the inside. He mentions six characteristics. They can be split into two sets of three.

1. The outward aspects

First there are the three outward observables of a man. He is to be *temperate*. Literally that means to be free from intoxicants. He is to have bodily appetites under control. He is to rule his desires, not let his desires rule him. In Crete Paul has made it plain that men are often 'evil brutes, lazy gluttons'. The modern picture of the beer-swilling womanizer as being a tough man is a lie. These are not strong men. They are weak. They are men who are slaves to their own sinful appetites, and are unable to break free. By contrast the word 'temperate' used here comes from a root which carries the idea of being self-possessed under all circumstances.

He is to be *worthy of respect*. Literally the mature Christian man is to be a serious man. That does not mean that he must be a gloomy introvert incapable of having any fun. But it does mean that he never allows fun to go beyond the proper boundaries. There is a weightiness about his character which remains even in lighter moments. That weightiness of character brings a sense of gentle dignity which inspires confidence. Others who are with him feel protected and safe. This enables him to have a positive influence for good on others. There is a solidity and commitment to what is right which inspires younger men to secretly say to themselves, 'I want to be like him.'

He is to be *self-controlled*. The word used here refers particularly to the mind and to thought. He is to be a sensible man; someone known for sound judgement. He may not be an intellectual, but he is full of common sense. He is not a man who pretends to know the answer when he doesn't. He is not a rash man. He is guided by a sensible humility.

So the mature Christian is not some over-the-top, super-spiritual extrovert. Though his Christianity may have something of a mystical side, incomprehensible to the unbeliever,

an unseen communion with Jesus, yet he is very much a man
with his feet on the ground.

Temperance, weightiness of character, self-control — are
these our aims in life, men? Are these on our agenda as we seek
God in prayer to shape us into the mature Christian men he
would have us be?

Now the great thing about such characteristics in a Christian man is that they must be real. These attributes are to come
from the heart and not to be in any way a mask, or a hypocritical
show for others to see. They are based on a sound inner
spiritual life. This leads us to the second set of characteristics
which Paul desires Titus to seek to inculcate in the Christian
males, as marks of maturity.

2. *The inner life*

So secondly, there are three characteristics of the inner life of
a Christian man listed here. Paul tells Titus that the older men
are to be 'sound in faith, in love and in endurance'. This list is
a variation of the three great New Testament Christian virtues
of 'faith, hope and love'. Faith and love are there in our list, and
endurance can be seen as the practical side of hope.

What brings a joyful weightiness and dignity to a man's
character? The answer is: 'When through faith in Christ Jesus
he is in touch with the weight of God in his holy glory!' A man
whose eyes of faith constantly see the King of kings cannot but
be affected. Something of God's majestic glory rubs off on him,
just as Moses' face shone after God had shown him his glory.

What brings temperance and self-possession to a man
rather than brutish gluttony or self-absorbed loveless introver-
sion? When a man has drunk deeply of the holy love of God
for mankind at Calvary, and so been transformed into a lover
of mankind himself. The apostle Paul himself had come from
being a narrow-hearted Pharisaical persecutor of the church to

being the large-hearted servant of God, so that he could say, 'Christ lives in me', because he had come to know the profundity of the fact that 'The Son of God ... loved me and gave himself for me' (Gal. 2:20).

What brings patient endurance into a man's character which perseveres in doing good, no matter how tough the circumstances? The answer is: 'When his eyes are set, not ultimately on this world, but on the life to come.' Again, Paul himself had met the risen Lord Jesus on the road to Damascus. He had seen the reality of eternal life, and in Christ Jesus that same hope is set before us. Then we are able to say with conviction that the sufferings of this present time are not worth comparing with the glory which awaits us (Rom. 8:18), and we are given strength to endure. The inner life of faith, hope and love shapes the outward man.

It is worth noting here that the assumption behind the qualities which Paul looks for in a mature Christian man indicate that Paul's idea of the Christian life is not one of continual triumph and comparative ease. The Christian life is a tough life, which requires grit and endurance as well as faith and love. There is much talk these days about the triumphant power of the Holy Spirit in the Christian life. But very often we misconstrue the nature of the Spirit's power. Often it is a power which enables us not to be free of suffering, but to endure it (2 Tim. 1:8). The power of the Spirit, properly understood, flows from the cross of Jesus (John 19:34), is released by the message of the cross and empowers us to deny ourselves, take up the cross and follow the Lord Jesus.

In the 1980s the TV news presenter Anna Ford was involved in making a documentary about men. She interviewed, I understand, some 120 men from all walks of life and levels of society, from judges to miners and everything in between. Asked about what she found, she said she felt depressed because not one man she had talked to seemed to have any real purpose in life. Asked what was needed by men she replied with great insight that 'the outer man' and the 'inner man' needed to come together, which, she said, 'I suppose means finding God'. Now what she meant by that remark, and what she identifies as 'God', I do not know. But actually she said more than she probably knew. According to what we have seen in these verses, she was spot on. True masculinity is about an outward, loving, dignified strength which is based on a healthy inner spiritual life. To neglect our prayers is to neglect our manhood. To neglect our walk with God is the sure way for our masculinity to degenerate into unbridled oafishness or into religious hypocrisy. It is when a man's inner life is pollinated with Christian faith, hope and love that the flower of loving strength and true manhood blooms in his life. That is why a man's devotional life is of such importance.

Younger men (2:6-8)

'Similarly, encourage the young men to be self-controlled. In everything set them an example by doing what is good. In your teaching show integrity, seriousness and soundness of speech that cannot be condemned, so that those who oppose you may be ashamed because they have nothing bad to say about us.'

In the original language of the New Testament, there is no full stop at the end of verse 6. The command to encourage young men to be self-controlled flows right into the idea of Titus setting an example in everything. So these verses (2:7-8) can be taken as giving a place to start in Christian teachers helping young men to be self-controlled. It hardly needs saying that in the permissive, self-indulgent moral climate of a place like Crete, where to give in to any and every temptation was seen as the normal thing to do, such a virtue as self-control was of prime importance to young men. It remains just as important for young Christian men today.

The word *'self-control'* used here is the same word as was used of older men in verse 2, and refers first of all to having a sensible attitude of mind. The mind is the control room of the man. So if there is a self-controlled mind, the behaviour will follow. That is the key. Men are gifted with more physical strength, usually, than women. But that strength needs to be rightly channelled and controlled, in order to be used for good. How can we define self-control? Self-control can be thought of as the ability to discern and see the importance of the godly goal in a situation and to choose that goal over against competing desires and concerns. It involves being able to see and choose right over against the temptation to sin. It involves sometimes the ability to postpone immediate pleasure in order to get on with work that needs to be done. It requires strength. But that strength needs direction; thus the ability to discern and see the importance of the godly goal.

A Scripture example of such self-control occurs in the story of David in 1 Samuel 26. God had promised him the throne of Israel, and had rejected King Saul. However, as yet David had not come to the throne and was suffering persecution from the jealous and deranged Saul. In one incident as Saul is pursuing David, he and his men camp for the night near to David. Abishai and David are able to creep into the king's camp and take Saul's spear and water jug. While they are there, and the guards are asleep, Abishai encourages David to let him kill Saul: 'You know it is God's will for you to be on the throne, take your opportunity!' But David says 'No'. He replies that no one can strike the Lord's anointed and do right. Here David discerns the godly goal. Even though the opportunity is there before him, he must do right in the sight of God above all else. He lays aside the competing desire for a quick escape from persecution and an easy ascent to the throne. He can see how important it is to walk in a way that is pleasing to God. What use is it to have a quick end to persecution if he comes under God's displeasure? He lays aside immediate short-term gains for righteous long-term goals. He is God-centred rather than self-centred. Here is the heart of self-control.

Now the emphasis here in Titus is on growing young men to maturity, to the full-bloom of self-controlled Christian manhood. How is that to be done? Paul's instructions to Titus include three vital ingredients.

1. Encourage them

'Encourage the young men to be self-controlled.' The word for encouragement is often used in connection with the Holy Spirit. He is the one who comes alongside to stimulate and to comfort us. Young men learn through the friendship of older men in the congregation. Many young men go to seed for lack of a mature Christian man taking interest in them and coming alongside them. Often young people lack confidence. They need someone to gently correct them when they are on the wrong track and to show appreciation when they have done something well. Sadly, young men in our churches are often sat on by older leaders and never given any opportunity to develop their talents. This can lead to discouragement, resentment and problems in the church. Older men need to nurture younger men. In the matter of self-control, often younger men have issues in their lives which need airing in a heart-to-heart talk with a more mature man. The more mature Christian needs to be unshockable and able to share his own experiences. He can show what he has learned from his mistakes as well as his successes. There can be a warm but firm directing of young men along the right lines in a way that puts heart into them to follow the path of self-control. Self-control is never fashionable in an ungodly world. Young men need help, understanding and encouragement.

2. Be an example to them

Titus is a man who is younger than Paul. He is a younger man who has made tremendous headway as a Christian. Such people can provide excellent role-models for young men to pattern their lives on. Young men learn when they can see what is being taught lived out in practice in someone else's life. Titus is to set an example in **'doing what is good'**. Christlike deeds of love do challenge and brush off on others. The story of the prisoner-of-war camp on the River Kwai with which we started the chapter underlines that. Young men will not be helped by older men who are merely armchair Christians. They will be helped by men who live out their Christianity in good works of love, sacrifice, prayer and evangelism.

Titus is also to be an example in integrity and soundness of speech. Often foolish talk, especially among young men, can degenerate into hurtful, insensitive remarks. Titus is to set a pattern for good.

His good example is to be such that **'those who oppose you may be ashamed because they have nothing bad to say about us'**. Paul may be referring here to the false teachers, or to those in the congregation who may be rebellious against the godly lifestyle Titus is seeking to nurture in the churches. Either way, exemplary living has a powerful effect on people's consciences for good. This provides another reason for young Christians to learn self-control, lest by their actions they bring shame on the gospel. 'You have done that, and you are meant to be the Christian in the family!' say our unconverted relatives. How such a statement hurts! And often it hurts so much because we know they are right, and we, by our actions, have hindered them in accepting Christ. Here is a prime motive to learn 'self-control'. Think what will be the result of your action. Look beyond immediate gratification. Discern the godly goal and see its importance.

3. Expound the gospel to them

We have seen that the opening verse of the chapter underlines that the lifestyle of godliness flows out of the gospel. Self-control, part of the fruit of the Spirit, is rooted in the gospel. Here in verse 8, Paul exhorts Titus to show integrity in his teaching and soundness of speech. His teaching is to be healthy, pure, free from error and false teaching. The pure gospel has its own influence for good, to shape all people, including the young men in becoming mature believers.

Often the reason men do not develop to maturity as Christians, and hide for ever behind their masks, is because they have either never accepted Christ, or they have accepted him, but have never fully understood what the gospel is saying to them in all its grace.

Many men look at Christianity and the lifestyle of godliness and conclude, 'I could never keep it up.' That is the reason many of them give for not coming to Christ. Often it is an honest reason. They feel they would fail. Others look at the men of Scripture history and say, 'Yes, but I could never be like that.' In a world of redundancy and militant feminism men often lack confidence today. They have been made to feel useless in an ultra-competitive society. 'Look at me,' they say to themselves. 'I know what I am really like. I know the depth of my own sexual weaknesses, my pride, my self-doubts. I could never be like the holy men of the Bible.'

But the gospel replies, 'Don't be silly! Look at the Bible. Take a long look at those biblical characters. God deals with real men, not plaster saints. He cares for men like you.'

Think of David. If we consider the beginnings of David's story we get the impression that his father Jesse did not think too much of him. When the prophet Samuel is coming to honour the house with his visit, Jesse assembles all the family, but leaves David out with the sheep. Couldn't he have hired someone else to do that for the big day? How that young David might well have felt hurt by such a rejection! Are you a hurt man? Are you someone who as a youngster felt misused and rejected and you have carried the chip on your shoulder ever since? David was put down by his father, and later by his older brothers as he bravely volunteered to fight Goliath (1 Sam. 17). He was despised by others, but it was just this young man that God chose to be anointed as king! The world may despise us, but God chooses us.

Think of Samson, with all his lustful temptations. Think of Gideon, with his compulsive fears. Think of Peter with all his inborn foolish exhibitionism. Yet God takes hold of such men, and uses them, and they come to know him despite their failures. God covers their sins and transforms their lives.

Men, God knows you and your weaknesses better than you do, and he loves you. His love calls you to repentance. His love calls you away from your pride. He calls you to take off your mask of pretence, with which you try to fool other people, and come into his grace. It is God's grace, the knowledge of his free forgiveness and love, which enables a man to be at peace with himself and find strength to live a life of loving dignity and goodness.

John Knox was a great champion of the biblical gospel in Scotland during the sixteenth-century Reformation against the error of Roman Catholicism. As soon as he preached his first sermon in the Castle of St Andrews people said, 'Other men sawed the branches off the Papistry. This man lays his axe to the trunk of the tree.' It was true. He was a fearless man for the cause of the gospel.

Mary Queen of Scots came to the throne with the intention of imposing her Catholicism on Scotland. But Knox opposed her. 'Aren't you afraid to stand before Mary Queen of Scots and say the things you do?' people asked Knox. John Knox is said to have replied along these lines: 'Why should I be afraid of an earthly queen when I have been two hours this morning on my knees face to face with the King of kings, in prayer and in his Word?' There is strength. There is self-control. There is the inner man and the outer man at one in God.

We are not all called to be firebrands like John Knox, but the secret of his courage is the secret that Christian men, whether old or young, need to rediscover.

1. This table is taken from Graham Twelftree, *Drive Home the Point,* Monarch Publications, 1994.

5.
The pattern of godly womanhood

Please read again Titus 2:1-8

Paul is commanding Titus to instruct the Christians in the newly formed churches on the island of Crete in closing the gap between what they profess to believe and how they actually live as Christians. The apostle is insisting that Christians be trained in the lifestyle which is consistent with the gospel, flowing out of the good news of eternal life in Christ. He exhorts Titus: 'You must teach what is in accord with sound doctrine' (2:1), and what he is to teach is instruction for practical godly living, as the subsequent verses show.

In the last chapter we saw something of what those instructions were for men. Now it is the turn of the women. What does it mean to be a godly woman? This is what Paul commands his right-hand man Titus to teach in parallel with what he is to teach the men: **'Likewise, teach the older women to be reverent in the way they live, not to be slanderers or addicted to much wine, but to teach what is good. Then they can train the younger women to love their husbands and children, to be self-controlled and pure, to be busy at home, to be kind, and to be subject to their husbands, so that no one will malign the word of God.'**

Emphasis on family

What strikes us very forcefully, especially as we look at these verses through modern eyes, is what seems to be Paul's concentration on — some would say obsession with — marriage and homemaking when he speaks about the women. Why is that? What is the reason that domestic concerns appear to dominate?

There are two things to be said. First, the dominance of domestic concern is not because Paul believed that all women must marry. In other places in the New Testament, 1 Corinthians 7 for example, Paul teaches that to be single is a perfectly good way of life for either men or women if they have been gifted by God for singleness. That gift, which Paul views as a spiritual gift along with other charismata, includes the ability to be content socially and to remain celibate as a single person. In many ways there is an advantage in singleness which Paul is happy for Christians to exploit. It is not the worldly advantage of staying single in order to have freedom from responsibilities and to indulge sinful tendencies. Rather it is the spiritual advantage of being able to give oneself without distraction to the work of the Lord. Some people have such a gift and can be extremely effective for Christ. Paul himself was single and so able to give all his energies to spreading the gospel in a way which perhaps a married person could not. Hence the rationale for Christian singleness is different from the 'me'-centred rationale of our subjective modern world. But singleness is perfectly good, and handled rightly, can be very blessed by God. So the reason why Paul's instructions concerning women are heavily loaded towards marriage as he writes to Titus is not because Paul believes that marriage is an absolute must for all women. Marriage is right for some, but not necessarily for all.

Secondly, we have to say that Paul's emphasis on home and marriage for women in the letter to Titus seems to be coloured

by the situation on Crete. We were told in 1:11 that the false
teaching prevalent on Crete was undermining the family and
it seems that the women were being particularly affected by
this strand of error. This is confirmed by the fact that in the
verses we are looking at in this chapter the older women are to
be encouraged to 'train' the younger women to love their
families. In the original, the word 'train' can have the meaning
of 'to bring people back to their senses'. It is likely that the
whole attitude of many younger women towards family life
had been hijacked and soured by the errors and exaggerations
of the false teachers, so that even women who were already
married were made to feel discontented with their lot and were
looking for a way out of marriage.

In our own day a similar campaign has sometimes come
from the ultra-feminist lobby. In the United States not too
many years ago there was a widespread slogan: 'Motherhood
— Just say "No!"' It is easy to use pejorative language which
plays to the gallery of a self-centred generation, describing
babies as 'crying machines' and marriage as 'drudgery'. No
set of circumstances in this fallen world is perfect. Certainly
no situation is able to totally satisfy the sinful self. There are
inevitably disappointments and hardships for us all. We lament and sympathize with women who have been truly
mistreated in their marriages, but it is easy to turn everyday
disappointments and hardships into supposed evidence of
victimization and oppression when people's outlook is dominated by a self-centred view of personal freedom.

The kind of false teaching which was affecting the churches
towards the end of Paul's ministry was of the kind which
emphasized subjective spiritual experience, esoteric knowledge and developing personal religious awareness. Scholars
have called it an incipient form of gnosticism. If the false
teaching on Crete included this kind of emphasis we do not
have to look far to see how it could be used to undermine
marriage. A spirituality which emphasizes the need for hours

of meditation or perfect ceremonial purity, for personal religious growth and development, would inevitably militate
against the time and toil required for family life. It is interesting that in writing his first letter to Timothy Paul speaks of
false teachers who 'forbid people to marry' (1 Tim. 4:3) in
their search for some supposed spiritual development. Were
they teaching that marital relations and childbearing somehow
defile the woman's spirituality? If they were, this could well
be the explanation behind Paul's enigmatic statement in that
same letter of 1 Timothy that Christian 'women will be saved
through childbearing — if they continue in faith, love and holiness with propriety' (1 Tim. 2:15). Paul was not thinking of a
woman's eternal salvation being somehow connected with
childbirth, but rather saying that if a woman has faith in Christ,
childbirth does not in any way defile her or diminish her
spiritual standing before God. It is faith in Jesus alone which
matters whatever our situation. She will be saved in childbirth.

Thus it is probably along the lines of combating the anti-
family influence of the false teachers that Paul puts the home
and marriage so high on the agenda as he writes to Titus
concerning how to instruct the Christian women in godly
living. This is why in the first instance family and marriage
dominate Paul's priorities for the Cretan women.

As with his instructions to the men, Paul is concerned for
both older and younger people. Let us begin by looking at his
instructions for the older women.

Older women (2:3)

**'Likewise, teach the older women to be reverent in the way
they live, not to be slanderers or addicted to much wine,
but to teach what is good.'** He gives four instructions, two
positives and two negatives.

1. A reverent way of life

The godly mature woman is to be reverent in the way she lives (2:3). In the ancient world there were many temples dedicated to various supposed 'gods'. Many such temples were served by priestesses. They were often specially dressed, trained in deportment, taught how to serve their god and how to advise visitors to the temple to seek the god. Within the confines of the temple they acted as befitted the 'holy' place, with a self-deprecating submissive respect for the god in whose presence they were.

That is the kind of picture Paul takes up here as he commands the mature Christian woman to be reverent. She is a priestess of the true God, in the sense that all Christians are made a 'royal priesthood' belonging to God (1 Peter 2:9). She has access to God through Jesus Christ, which unbelievers do not have. She is clothed and acceptable in the seamless robe of Christ's righteousness, which covers all our sins. She is a chosen person set aside to the service of God. And the particular slant which Paul emphasizes here is that an attitude of reverence towards God is not just appropriate to her for the priests of some 'temple' building, but for her approach to the whole of life. Reverence is to suffuse her total lifestyle. She is to be 'reverent in the way she lives', because in Christ all of life is now become our spiritual worship offered to God (Rom. 12:1-2). The Christian priestess lives in God's presence at all times, serving God. Her very body is a temple of the Holy Spirit (1 Cor. 6:19). Thus the Christian woman is called away from the slovenly and decadent ways of a world where there is no one to please but oneself. She is to live as one who has special access to the living and true God, and as befits one who is able to advise others how to find him in Christ.

2. No slander

That reverence which Paul is looking for is contrasted with the ways of ungodly women on Crete. The self-indulgent, indolent ways of Crete showed themselves in the women there in their being slanderers of other people. The Christian women are **'not to be slanderers'**, says Paul. There is something in the sinful self which delights to think the worst of others, and spread such things. What is thought of others in this vein is gossiped around. The sophisticated slur seems so witty even if there is little or no basis for it. This can be the mechanism which people use to enable them to feel better about themselves. If we can show others in a bad light, people may think better of us. It can simply be a vicious delight in bringing trouble on other people, or it can arise out of a desire to cause trouble for an enemy who is threatening our position. So it was that false, slanderous charges were brought against Jesus by the religious leaders of his day, who felt threatened by his popularity with the people. 'Avoid such slander,' says Paul to Christlike women.

3. No drunkenness

The lifestyle of godly reverence, suited to a sacred Christian priestess, is also incompatible with the drunkenness which affected many women in Crete. The Christian woman is **'not'** to be **'addicted to much wine'**. Often women's lives can be hard. They frequently carry deep hurts in their lives from the past. One way out for many women is the bottle. Such women speak of alcohol dulling the emotional pain of their lives and for a time putting a distance between themselves and their sorrows. The self-indulgent, loose attitudes of Crete thought nothing of drunkenness. How many homes have been ruined by mothers (or fathers) addicted to drink? This is not for the Christian. Yes, life can be hard, but we are to find all our consolation in the living Lord who loves us. In our modern world we must widen out this teaching concerning avoiding of addiction to include tranquillizers and drugs too. Here I am not talking about a proper medical use of prescribed pills, but an addiction to them. The addicted person is no longer in control of his or her life, but is ruled by that habit. 'Avoid such addiction,' says Paul to Christian women.

4. A teaching ministry

The reverent lifestyle for the mature Christian woman is to find a positive outlet in a teaching ministry. Paul is going on to commend the idea of older Christian women teaching and training the younger ones. If there is to be a habit, an addiction in the lives of the godly older women, it is to be the habit of coming alongside younger sisters in Christ and **'teach[ing] what is good'** (2:3).

Very probably some of the false teaching on Crete was of the type which taught that spirituality is all about ceremonial purity and esoteric knowledge (1:15-16). It would involve instructions: 'Do not touch this'; 'Don't soil yourself with that.' It would be antithetical to involvement in the mundane matters of life. As we have said, perhaps it was ideas of this kind which were leading Christian women away from the home and family.

By contrast, true spirituality is involved in daily life, bringing Christ into the everyday. So it is that the mature Christian priestess is to teach, by personal advice and active example, how to serve the Lord in everyday life and how, under his transforming hand, the mundane becomes blessed and glorious.

The task thy wisdom hath assigned
Oh, let me cheerfully fulfil,
In all my works thy presence find
And prove thy good and perfect will!

(Charles Wesley)

This teaching will include how to handle family life and to be pure and kind in all relationships. True spirituality is about being in the world though not of it. Christian maturity is to be deeply involved with the world and its people, not forever withdrawing from it in search of a personal spiritual high.

We have to say that this ministry of older women teaching the younger women is crucial for the modern church. It is crucial, not only because the outlook of the modern world leans in the direction of ignoring any biblical distinctions between the roles of men and women, but also for the simple reason that statistically there are more women than men in the church today. Though, as we have already seen, this cannot involve women in eldership, yet the church desperately needs this teaching ministry of godly, reverent mature Christian priestesses, qualified to teach and train younger women. The churches need to wake up to this fact and facilitate such ministry.

This leads us inevitably to ask the question: 'What are they to teach?' Paul deals with this subject as we turn our attention to the younger Christian women.

Younger women (2:4-5)

Having explained the qualities required in a mature Christian woman, Paul goes on to tell Titus that if those qualities are present, **'Then they can train the younger women to love**

their husbands and children, to be self-controlled and pure, to be busy at home, to be kind, and to be subject to their husbands...'

There are seven elements here. We could call them seven secrets of a successful wife. I do not think that these characteristics are meant to cover everything. I am sure that they are selected, as we have indicated already, to some extent with the Cretan situation of a morally corrupt, self-indulgent, society in mind. But nevertheless all these characteristics are required, in order to live consistently with the Word of God as a Christian wife (2:5).

Love for husbands and children

The first two characteristics which Paul highlights are found in the fact that younger women should be trained to love their husbands and to love their children. These are two separate aspects of love. Love for a husband is one thing. Love for children is something else. To be good in the area of one of these loves does not make up for a lack in the other area. Both are required for a family woman.

For our encouragement it should also be noted that according to Scripture love is something which can be learned. The younger women were to be 'trained' in it. Love is not the hit-or-miss, scratch-card gamble affair — 'either you've got it or you haven't' — which the world makes it out to be. With God's help, it can be learned. That means that marriages that have run into trouble can be repaired by the grace of God.

Self-control

Third in Paul's list for godly womanhood is self-control. In the subjective, morally permissive atmosphere of Crete, it is not surprising that this quality of self-control keeps cropping up in Paul's teaching for godly living. To be able to discern the godly goal and grasp its importance so as to choose the right path is needed just as much in women as in men. It is self-control, part of the Holy Spirit's fruit, which is essential to overcome temptation of all kinds.

The word used for self-control here is once again that word which refers particularly to the thought-life of a person. It is a word with the same root as the word Paul uses when he writes to Timothy that God gave us a spirit of power, of love and of self-discipline, or 'a sound mind' (2 Tim. 1:7). It is the sensible outlook that is required. The church needs level-headed women just as much as it needs level-headed men. In the book of Proverbs both the wife of noble character and wisdom itself are likened to rubies. 'Houses and wealth are inherited from parents, but a prudent wife is from the Lord' (Prov. 19:14).

Purity

Fourthly, the Christian woman is called to be pure. This should follow directly if a married woman loves her husband. However, in the complexity of our fallen human nature, it may not be as simple as that. And single women need to be reminded of sexual purity too. Thus Paul spells it out. Sexual purity always commends the gospel to other people, even though they scoff at purity for a Christian. To fall in this area is always a scandal in the eyes of the world. Sexual purity is a picture of the church's faithfulness to Christ the husband. Sexual purity keeps a person from a guilty conscience and later from feeling like used goods. Sexual impurity, whether before or after marriage, always runs the risk of damaging relations within marriage from then on. The question always stays: 'Can he/she really be trusted?'

Efficiency and kindness

Paul looks to the married Christian woman to be busy at home and to be kind. Although Scripture does not have a rigid rule, but allows for flexibility, generally it can be said that it sees work to provide for the family as the focus of a husband's orbit of life, while work within the family is the focus of the wife's orbit. It is the wife's feminine ability for nurture which turns a house into a home, with all the warmth which the word 'home' implies. This may not preclude a wife taking a job outside the home but it takes a great deal of effort on a wife's part.

For Paul, the trick is in the balancing of efficiency with kindness. It is possible for a house to be unkempt and therefore uncomfortable. It is possible for a wife to be so fussy about having a spotless house that she forgets that people are meant to live there. It is that balance of both a wife's toil and tenderness which brings joy and a sense of 'belonging' to even the most humble home.

Submission to husbands

Lastly, Paul, consistently with his teaching on marriage throughout his letters, looks for godly wives to be **'subject to their husbands'**. Marriage is a partnership of equals, but the different partners take different roles. The wife is to be intelligently submissive to her husband's humble leadership. Paul states it very starkly here, probably because of the rebellious attitude engendered by the false teaching on Crete. He is dealing with a vicious error which is threatening the stability of the family and therefore he has to be blunt. No doubt he is expecting Titus to fill out this teaching as Paul does elsewhere. He looks for Titus to set it in the context of the necessity of a husband's Christlike loving leadership, which is always exercised for the good of his bride rather than for himself, which makes his headship a blessing rather than a burden. Christ gave himself for his bride the church. In such a relationship there is a mutual submission as both husband and wife take on the roles which have been assigned them by Christ their Saviour.

Here, then, are seven key aspects of godliness for the Christian woman. They may not be fashionable in our day, but they still need to be taken seriously.

Having looked at the verses in this section of Titus, we need to highlight four lessons. There are three general principles and one which is specific to women.

Gospel lifestyle

All this teaching about the pattern of godliness for both men and women flows out of the gospel. It is both congruent with and learned from the good news of Jesus Christ. Paul's starting-point, remember, was to tell Titus, 'You must teach what is in accord with sound doctrine.'

Though the Gentile world of ancient days was often very corrupt, as in Crete, yet of course every individual has a conscience and hence a sense of what is noble and true as a way of life, even if they do not follow it themselves. Some commentators approach the teaching on the roles of men and women in this chapter as if what Paul was teaching was simply an attempt to commend the gospel to the ancient Gentile world by encouraging Christians to live according to the norms of what was looked on as 'respectable' or 'noble' by the world of that time. This would actually relativize Paul's teaching. If the ideas of respectability in the Gentile world changed, then Christian behaviour would change too in order to gain acceptance. It is important to see that this is not what Paul is saying here. He did not write to Titus, 'Teach what is in accord with current ideas of respectability,' but rather 'what is in accord with sound doctrine'. This roots the pattern for a godly lifestyle squarely into Christ and the world to come, not into the fashions of this current world or the fallible consciences of fallen people. It is not the world which should dictate Christian lifestyle, but the gospel.

This is underlined by the way Paul motivates both men and women to live a godly life. The women are to live the female godly lifestyle 'so that no one will malign the word of God' (2:5). Titus is to set an example of godly manhood to the younger men and teach with integrity so that 'those who oppose you may be ashamed because they have nothing bad to say about us' (2:8); in other words so that Titus can be seen to practise what he preaches. It is God who made male and female. It is God who ordained marriage and ordered the roles of marriage partners. For Christians to live otherwise is to undermine the Word of God and the gospel itself. It is to give live ammunition to the gospel's enemies. They are able to say, 'They say one thing, yet do something else.' This is the great danger of the gap between what we believe and how we behave.

For Paul the gospel and Christian lifestyle are all of a piece. The women will be trained to love their husbands and children. How are we to learn to love, even when a situation is less than ideal? The answer is from the gospel, from the love of God to sinners. Paul has emphasized self-control for both men and women. Why do we need to be self-controlled, sensible people? Because the gospel teaches us that though there is true joy in God and all his gifts, yet life is not a joke. We live in the light of eternity, either under the glow of heaven, or the shadow of hell. The gospel teaches a lifestyle of service. Men and women are to serve one another in love. The family man

and the family woman are despised by today's world. But if
Jesus himself has been subject to the Father in heaven, and has
gone there now to prepare a place for us, then being a homemaker is a high calling and not something to be despised. The
more we believe the biblical gospel, the more we will honour
and respect the role of wife and mother. Similarly, if Jesus has
given himself to death to save his bride the church, then to be
a loving husband who leads in such a way as to put the good
of his wife and family before his own good is not foolish but
truly noble.

The first lesson, then, is that although there is room for
some flexibility, the patterns of godly manhood and womanhood found here in Titus are bound up with the 'sound
doctrine' of the gospel.

Youth culture

The second lesson which we need to reflect on from these first
eight verses of Titus 2 concerns the orientation of our Western
culture at the present time. Since the 1950s a revolution has
taken place. Youth dominates. Our society idolizes being
young. This is inevitable in a world like ours which thinks only
in terms of this life. To be young is to be healthy and active and
without responsibilities. It is the time of our lives when we are
physically most attractive and all our choices and possibilities
for life are still before us. To be young is to be valuable; to be
old is to be worthless. So it is that in our day the old and the
elderly are often simply tolerated and more and more sidelined
from life. Today's church has followed suit, idolizing youth.

What we find in Paul's instructions to Titus is quite different. Older folk are people who are prized. They can be the very
spiritual treasury of the church. Of course, the church needs to
care for and encourage its young people, but the best way to do

that, says Paul, is by encouraging them to allow themselves to be taken under the wing of those who have been around a little longer than they have.

'Teach the older women... Then they can train the younger women' (2:3-4). Similarly with the men. The rationale behind this comes from the perspective of the gospel. This life is not all. We are bound for heaven in Christ. In following Jesus we are taking on the lifestyle, not of a passing period of time, but of eternity. It makes sense therefore for those who have been followers of Christ longer to teach those who are relatively new to the way of life. It makes sense because, whether we are old or young, we all have the same ultimate goal in mind. That goal is not a transitory happiness which is dependent on whatever passing fashions of the world may have captured our hearts and therefore could be very different for old and young. Our goal is a heavenly joy and a life which is eternal. So elderly Christians who are spiritually mature have much to teach us all. This calls for youngsters to be teachable and for older ones to have a loving interest in, and understanding of, young people and their world in order to truly help them.

Women of no compromise

In the verses which we have particularly looked at in this chapter Paul has concentrated on a wife's role in the home and family. What Paul is saying here to women who marry is: 'Don't compromise, make your home and family your priority; throw yourself into it; give it all you have got.'

For a society such as ours, which worships the concept of freedom of personal choice, such commitment is problematical. If to maintain personal choice is our highest priority then inevitably we shall have an attitude to life which seeks to keep as many options open as possible. We are back to the picture of the market-place and ourselves as the consumers who move among the stalls weighing up the possibilities. If we are those who worship personal freedom of choice, then what happens when that attitude becomes a state of mind with us? We must always seek to keep our options as open as possible. It leads to a generation of people who fight shy of commitment, for to be committed means to have chosen one option to the exclusion of others. What Paul is saying is: 'Don't be like that. If you have chosen marriage then go for it. Be committed to it totally.'

Let us be practical. Paul is not saying that married women must not work outside the house. That may be perfectly fine. But if work outside the home becomes a threat, or undermines the role of mother and homemaker, it is better to let the extra money go. If marriage and family are for you, then go for it. Put your whole energy into it as a Christian woman.

Reflect on these quotes: 'It is difficult to be married to someone who was married to her success and therefore not to me.' That was actor Elliott Gould in the *Radio Times*, speaking about his eight years of marriage to the actress and singer Barbara Streisand.

Actress Katherine Hepburn said in an interview, 'I'm not sure women can successfully pursue a career and be a mother at the same time. The trouble with women today is that they want everything. But no one can have it all. I haven't been handicapped by children. Nor have I handicapped children by bringing them into the world and going ahead with my career.'

Another actress, Joanne Woodward, has said this: 'My career has suffered because of the children, and my children have suffered because of my career. I've been torn and haven't been able to function fully in either arena. I don't know one person who does both successfully, and I know a lot of working mothers.'

Golda Meir, the great former prime minister of Israel, confessed that she had nagging doubts about the price her children had paid for her career. She said, 'You can get used to anything if you have to, even to feeling perpetually guilty.'

Paul's message to women who have chosen the high calling of wife, mother and homemaker is not to compromise, but to be totally committed to your family.

Self-denial

The last lesson again applies to us all. Obviously to be a wife and a mother is not easy. It requires self-denial. That is the same for husbands too, if they take seriously the responsibility of leading a family in a Christlike way. Self-denial is required for all genuine Christian living, whether we are married or single, as we seek to love and serve others in the different relationships of life. To a self-centred, self-indulgent society, the idea of self-denial is anathema. But actually it does lead to blessing. Jesus said, 'Unless a grain of wheat falls to the ground and dies, it remains only a single seed. But if it dies, it produces many seeds. The man who loves his life will lose it, while the man who hates his life in this world will keep it for eternal life' (John 12:24-25). Such living only makes sense because of the gospel. It is teaching that is in accord with sound doctrine. Those who deny self and are prepared to 'lose their lives' in the service of Christ and others (be it literally in martyrdom or metaphorically in sacrificial ministry) reap a harvest of character, life and influencing others for Christ. How many great Christian pioneers of the past have owed their conversion to godly Christian mothers! One thinks of Timothy (2 Tim. 1:5; 3:15), of Augustine of Hippo and of the Wesleys. Those who give themselves reap a wonderful harvest.

But those who try to save their lives are disappointed, left alone in the end, like the woman whose epitaph on her tombstone read like this:

Here lie the bones of Nancy Jones.
For her life held no terrors:
She lived an old maid,
She died an old maid,
No hits, no runs, no errors.

Being an old maid is not a matter of age, gender or marital status. Many elderly single women are true heroines in Christ, full of good works and service. No. Old-maidishness is not about age or gender. Rather it is a matter of outlook. Some of the worst old maids I have met have been young men! Old-maidishness is a matter of perspective. It is about always protecting yourself, never being willing to venture yourself purely for the good of others. It is about 'keeping yourself to yourself', rather than looking out for the interests of others. The great lesson of true Christian faith is that it is in flinging our lives away in the believing service of God and those in need that we find ourselves transformed and liberated.

You would think that if you pursue the process of dying you would die, but in Jesus, you don't. Like Jesus we find it is the other way round. He who went willingly to death on the cross for us is risen and alive for evermore. This is the way it is with eternal life. It is in dying to self that we live.

Sadly, the converse is also true. Those singles who are single through a pursuit of selfish ambition, forever protecting their own personal space in life, frequently end as lonely people. Those men I know who insist on their rights and never 'give in' to their wives because they are trying to protect their male egos are invariably underneath the ones who are uncertain about their manhood and their self-worth. Those women who 'keep themselves to themselves' rarely find joy in it. Women who lavish care on themselves and who spend hours on their own appearance, or their health, or their diet, are invariably the insecure and anxious ones beneath the surface. Life abundant eludes them all.

Christ has given us the key to be liberated into life, through a faith in him which follows him.

Through losing ourselves, we find ourselves. Through denying ourselves, we find true satisfaction. Through dying daily we find life. Everything else is suicide.

6.
The pattern of godly work

Please read Titus 2:9-10

Titus is a book concerned with closing the gap, the disparity between what Christians maintain they believe and the way they actually live their lives at a practical level. In the modern world it is probably true that the gap is nowhere more apparent than in the workplace. Sadly, frequently Christians are one thing at church, but really quite different at work. The spiritual atmosphere of church and the secular atmosphere of the workplace result in a kind of Jekyll and Hyde Christianity for the modern believer.

Perhaps inadvertently, this rather two-faced attitude is summed up in an interview which Ray Kroc, founder of MacDonald's Hamburgers, gave to the *New York Times* towards the end of his life. He said this: 'I speak of faith in MacDonald's as if it were a religion. I believe in God, family and MacDonald's — and in the office that order is reversed.' And in the modern workplace there are pressures on people to do just that, to all intents and purposes to encourage them to forget their moral principles and their faith in God, in the pragmatic pursuit of profits and efficiency for the company. So it is that the gap opens up.

In writing to Titus, Paul is very concerned about how false teaching is damaging 'households' (1:11) on the island of Crete. In New Testament times, slaves were part of many households. So it is that in addressing his subject Paul addresses the matter of how Titus should teach these household servants who were very much part of the contemporary culture: **'Teach slaves to be subject to their masters in everything, to try to please them, not to talk back to them, and not to steal from them, but to show that they can be fully trusted, so that in every way they will make the teaching about God our Saviour attractive.'**

Obviously we live in a somewhat different culture from that of first-century Crete, but as Paul addresses the matter of the attitude of Christian slaves to their work, there are unchanging principles which we are to learn from, for our lives in the modern situation.

An objection

However, before we come to that, I want to answer a question which may have arisen in our minds. In Titus 2 Paul sets out the behaviour he requires of different groups within the church-cum-household — young, old, men, women, slaves. As we have seen in the previous chapter, it is sometimes argued that what is taught here simply reflects the cultural approach to these matters found in the society of Paul's time, and that the apostle is simply asking for conformity to the accepted norms and practices of the day so that the gospel will not be damaged by appearing to be too radical in the eyes of respectable pagans. This argument is then pressed by saying that if we try to maintain a differentiation between male and female roles as a biblical norm, rather than something which is purely a cultural matter, then we shall end up having to say that slavery too is a biblical norm. If we do not maintain that we should have slavery today on the basis of Titus 2:9-10 then we should not argue from the rest of Titus 2 about maintaining a differentiation of roles for men and women, husbands and wives. In a nutshell, it is argued that the existence of slavery and the submission of slaves to their masters and the different roles of husbands and wives stand or fall together. How can you argue that one is an absolute biblical norm and not the other? It is a fair question, but it is based on a false premise. Paul deals with men, women and slaves together here, not because they are theologically related to the gospel in precisely the same way, but simply because they all formed part of the 'household' in the ancient world. But let us look at the objection. The Bible, and our passage in Titus in particular, provides us with very clear answers. We will note both the general answer and the specific answer from this passage.

1. The general answer

Generally, of course, within the Bible as a whole the answer lies in the fact that marriage, and the structure of relationship within marriage, goes right back to the 'very good' creation of God. Right from the start Adam was meant to exercise a loving headship over Eve, in that he was responsible for them both in a way in which she was not. That is why throughout Scripture, though Eve took of the forbidden fruit first, yet the responsibility for the Fall of mankind is placed squarely on Adam's shoulders, not on Eve. 'Sin entered the world through one man' (Rom. 5:12). 'As in Adam all die...' (1 Cor. 15:22). So the husband's headship, which also reflects the headship of Christ over the church, goes right back to creation.

By contrast, slavery was not a part of the 'very good' of creation, but is consequent upon the Fall. Indeed the very effects of the Fall are spoken of in terms of slavery. Humanity was brought into the bondage of sin and death (Rom. 6:17).

So it is that the two are very different and cannot be argued in parallel. Thus, elsewhere in the New Testament, although

Paul is always quick to defend and support the marriage relationship, by contrast he encourages slaves that, though they should seek to be content with their lot in life, given a proper opportunity to gain their freedom, they should take it (1 Cor. 7:21). Paul did not see these matters as standing or falling together and neither should we.

The answer in this passage

Specifically from Titus 2, it is interesting to note the different language which Paul uses in arguing the two cases. Though the motive for being a good marriage partner or a trustworthy slave is the gospel (2:1), Paul makes a definite distinction between why loving submission should be pursued in the two cases.

The wife's submission to her husband is argued 'so that no one will malign the word of God' (2:5). The slaves' helpfulness is urged 'so that in every way they will make the teaching about God our Saviour attractive' (2:10). The first is to keep the gospel from negative comments. The second is to secure for the gospel positive comments.

If a Christian wife throws off the idea of respect and submission to her husband, that is inconsistent with the gospel, for the marriage relationship was part and parcel of God's good creation, and the Christian church is saved by the very fact that Christ is our Husband and, as our Head, took responsibility for us and atoned for sin in our place. To throw over the idea and practice of headship in marriage impinges on the very essence of the gospel and thus opens the Word of God up to being maligned.

By contrast the slave's helpfulness to his master is motivated by a desire to make the gospel attractive. The word translated 'attractive' here is one from which we get our word 'cosmetic'. While disrespect for his master, or any other

human being, would bring the gospel into disrepute (1 Tim.
6:1), a slave's positive helpfulness to his master falls into the
category of going the extra mile. Given the cultural situation
of slavery, then willing submission and a positive desire to
please is a cosmetic, an extra-enhancement, for the gospel in
the eyes of the master. 'If even in their unfortunate position as
slaves, this good news of Jesus gives these people self-respect
and hope, it really must have something powerfully worth-
while to it.'

So, although both these attitudes flow from the gospel
itself, they do so in different ways, with different motivations.
Thus you cannot say that slavery and the defence of separate
male and female roles stand or fall together. Slavery is a
cultural matter, and we are glad that people like William
Wilberforce worked hard for its abolition. The distinction
between the roles of the two equal partners, male and female,
however, is fundamental to biblical faith.

Having dealt with that objection we now turn to consider
our verses in their own right. What can we learn, as Paul
addresses the situation of first-century Christian slaves, about
how to close the gap between faith and behaviour in the
workplace at the close of the twentieth century? The verses fall
naturally under two headings — the aim and the approach in
the workplace.

The aim in the workplace

We begin at the end for once. The aim in the slaves' service,
says Paul, is to be **'that in every way they will make the
teaching about God our Saviour attractive'**.

In verse 9, Paul has said, **'Teach slaves to be subject to
their masters.'** The word used for the slave's submission here
is a heavier and stronger word than Paul generally uses in

dealing with this issue, as in Ephesians 6 or Colossians 3. It may once again reflect the results of the false teaching in Crete. It may well be an echo of the fact that the false teaching was 'ruining whole households' (1:11), in the sense that it had been provoking Christian slaves into discontent and adopting aggressive attitudes and even rebellion against their masters. Remember that, though some slave owners were oppressive and unjust, often a master could be a kind man who almost treated his slaves as part of the family. There was rebellion brewing. But Paul is saying a firm 'No!' He is spelling out that this is not the Christlike way. Rather the aim and motivation for Christian slaves is to behave 'so that in every way they will make' the gospel 'attractive'.

Today, obviously, our situation is very different. Certainly in the Western world we do not live with circumstances of slavery within the workplace. The relationship between employer and employee is on a different footing, with a contract and legal obligations on both sides. The change from a society of slavery to one of contractual arrangements which are more just has in many ways been brought about by the prevalence of Christian principles in society in former years.

Though our situation may have changed markedly from that of the first-century slave, yet surely our aim in the workplace should remain the same — to make the teaching about God our Saviour attractive.

Let me sharpen this up a little. Our aim at work must not just be to please the boss, or even to witness in the hope of winning people to Christ. We should have a larger aim. The great need is to recapture the spirit of the workplace for Christ. The bigger vision is that Christians set out to change the ethos of the business world.

You see, why is our witness at work so hard? Why is our Christianity (if we have the courage to reveal it to our colleagues) basically ignored at the place of business? The reason is because the workplace in the twentieth century, and as we stand on the brink of the twenty-first, has been taken over by a totally secular outlook. Christian ethics are viewed as futile, if not dangerous to the health of a business in the cut and thrust of commerce and industry. God is viewed as irrelevant in the market-place.

We need to be reminded that this did not use to be the case. Our capitalist system in the West can be traced back to deep roots in the Reformation. Historians have endlessly discussed the so-called Protestant work-ethic which grew up with the rise of biblical Christianity with Luther and Calvin. Our forefathers had an outlook which saw the workplace in terms of the mandate given to mankind by God to subdue and nurture creation, and to explore and manage its potentialities to the glory of God and the good of mankind. This was once the driving force of both business and technology. In many ways, the workplace could rightly be seen as a place of worship, where people's skills, strength and inventiveness were offered in service to Christ. 'Whatever you do, work at it with all your heart, as working for the Lord, not for men... It is the Lord Christ you are serving' (Col. 3:23-24).

Historically, with the liberal attacks upon Scripture and the rise of an evolutionary explanation of the world, the aim of working and building a great society to the glory of God faded. Instead it was replaced by the secularized myth of 'progress'. In the earlier part of our century socialist ideas reigned. Those who advocated working to produce justice and equality in the workplace and society saw no need for God. The goal was a technological Utopia, with wealth and opportunity distributed equally to all. This vision is based on the false assumption of the essential goodness of humanity and willingness to share, and has faltered. Its most obvious demise has been seen in the oppressive results of Communism and its consequent cata-strophic collapse in Eastern Europe. The aim in the workplace to work for a Utopian future society did not motivate people. It did not produce justice and joy. It has failed.

The socialist dream having faded, it is now being replaced by the myth of individual materialism. The aim in the workplace has now no wider vision than to accumulate for self and one's nearest and dearest. This means that the market-place actually becomes a jungle, where the rule is that of everyone for him or herself. Though this is the current philosophy of the workplace, and finds wide acceptance, pandering as it does to the inherent sinful selfishness of human beings, this too will ultimately prove destructive. No man is an island. We do live in a society. Yet for self-interest to dominate our business and cultural outlook is inevitably antithetical to society.

The seminal economist of the eighteenth century Adam Smith argued that encouraging the rich to get richer would not damage society for as they got richer they would inevitably employ more servants and buy more services and so more poor folk would have jobs and not go hungry. The rich were said in this way to be led by an 'invisible hand' without knowing it, which advanced the interests of society.

But in our advanced economy this argument is no longer sound. We have moved into a technological age where machines, computers and gadgets of all kinds have drastically lessened the need for people to be employed in service industries. Also our economic advance has raised the expectations of ordinary people above that of the eighteenth century when the aim was to be employed so as simply not to go hungry. Ordinary people look for opportunities for achievement and fulfilment in life beyond the subsistence level. They wish to exercise their freedom to choose and make a life for themselves which dead-end jobs or living on the dole cannot provide.

The aim of ever greater business and economic efficiency is indifferent to the needs of society. It is prepared to see large

numbers of people made redundant. These folk will understandably form a restless underclass who may well feel disen-
franchised from society and therefore not averse to antisocial
behaviour. We are already seeing this in the behaviour of
young people who feel that society holds no future for them.
Crime statistics are related to unemployment statistics.

As we have said, we live in a society in which personal
freedom of choice is idolized. Money brings freedom to
choose what you want. Thus nothing higher than individual
materialism is the great motivator of our times. This being the
case, government is focused on keeping taxation and therefore
spending on public services as low as possible. But it is such
public services which in many ways provide the glue for
keeping our society together. If a society is not interested in
looking after its various members, or is only concerned to
spend the absolute minimum on looking after them, then it will
not be long before many people decide to opt out of society and
to live differently. That different way of living may well be
outside the law of the land and detrimental to the stability of
society.

Our society can only be set on a firm footing as the aims of
society and of the workplace are radically changed. The
prevalent visions of our century have been based on mistaken
ideas of humanity. The socialist dream of working for a just
Utopia miscalculated on the comradeship of fallen human
beings. Thus it became unworkable. The dream of individual
materialism miscalculates in thinking that giving personal
selfishness its full rein can produce a stable society. It cannot.
It leads to the disintegration of society. What is needed is for
the Christian vision to be recaptured. Christianity is realistic
about sinfulness in humanity, but has the answer in 'God our
Saviour'. He is the God who is able to redeem both the
individual and the structures of society in which the individual
is placed.

As Christians, we need once again 'in every way [to] make the teaching about God our Saviour attractive'. We need to recapture society's vision, and basic to that is recapturing the spirit of the workplace for the Lord. Our aim must be to show people that Christ is not just relevant on Sundays, but during the whole week. (We may have strayed some way from the details of our text in Titus, but not from the spirit of our verses.) We need to show that the application of Christian principles of honesty and service in the workplace is in the long term best for society, best for the company and its staff, best for the individual. That should be our ambition.

Now I realize that this is an enormous agenda. But this, it seems, is a vital area for seeing true change in our society. So long as Christianity is left outside the workplace, then society can easily dismiss it as privatized religion which is not actually relevant to real life. It is a key matter to bring Christ into the workplace, because in so many ways it is business and commerce (rather than overt godless philosophies) which are the engine of the secularization which we lament in our modern world.[1]

Beyond this principle of the Christian's aim at work, Paul also writes to Titus concerning how to behave in the workplace. This is highlighted in verse 9 and the beginning of verse 10.

The approach in the workplace (2:9-10)

'Teach slaves to be subject to their masters in everything, to try to please them, not to talk back to them, and not to steal from them, but to show that they can be fully trusted...'

Slavery in New Testament times could be a terrible oppression, but often masters were reasonable people and in

some senses slavery could be seen as the first-century equivalent of a welfare system which benefited the rich and provided
work and maintenance for the unfortunate poor. The Christian
slave, says Paul, is to be subject to his master, and to do so in
a way which commends Christ. What did this mean in practice? Paul gives four commands, with two positives and two
negatives.

1. Try to please the master (2:9)

Pleasing the master would mean first of all carrying out his
instructions satisfactorily and doing their best for him. This
obviously would usually mean exertion and hard work. Slaves
were generally motivated to work well by the promise that
perhaps by so doing they would earn their freedom. But as we
shall see, although the Christian was not to pass over an
opportunity for freedom if proffered, he was to have a different
motivation.

2. Do not talk back (2:9)

The attitude of slaves generally would have been sulky and
surly towards their masters. For a slave to be rebellious is
understandable from the human point of view. Often that
rebelliousness would express itself in sarcastic comments
uttered under the breath. But the Christian slave was not to
question his orders, except in the situation where he was called
to go against God's laws (Acts 5:29). And even in such a cause
the Christian is called to speak to his master respectfully.

Such instructions come right to us in the modern workplace. How easy it is to join in the 'them' and 'us' attitude of
employees towards employers, and to indulge in gossip and
criticism! This is not for the Christian in the workplace.

3. Do not steal (2:10)

The eighth commandment of the Decalogue applies in the workplace just as much as anywhere else. Many slaves in the ancient world were entrusted with their master's business interests and had great opportunity for theft of various kinds. Now, as then, the Christian is to shun such temptations. Remember it was Judas who was greedy for money. To be a thief is to betray our Lord. If we are in personal need, we are to turn to prayer, not to purloining that which is not rightfully ours.

4. Prove they can be fully trusted (2:10)

The superb example of Joseph is set before us in the Old Testament Scripture of a slave who was both wonderfully competent and absolutely trustworthy. While he worked for Potiphar he so commended himself to his master that 'He left in Joseph's care everything he had; with Joseph in charge, he did not concern himself with anything except the food he ate' (Gen. 39:6). Whether it was matters of finance or getting things done, in everything Joseph could be fully trusted. This is the kind of example all Christian workers are to seek to emulate. It is the path of blessing in the workplace.

The Christian in the workplace, then, is to be a hard-working, pleasant, friendly, honest, willing person. That is the way to win friends for the gospel. That is the way for the gap to be closed in the workplace.

Where can we find motivation, strength and resources to act like that? Surely it is in verse 10, through a living faith in 'God our Saviour'. Paul means us to make the connection. It is by believing in Christ that we are equipped for the problems of the workplace. By believing that he loves us we are able to draw on the resources of his Holy Spirit to strengthen us. By believing in Christ our Saviour who rose from the dead, we can see that despite our earthly circumstances, which like those of the first-century slave may be other than we would have them, there is an eternal future for us and therefore we have hope. By believing that Christ became a servant/slave for us and went to the cross for our sins when we deserved no such love, and he deserved no such death, we have an inspirational role-model to follow in our difficulties. By believing in Christ, we have a Friend who has lived in this world, sweated in the carpenter's shop to meet deadlines for his customers, and is able to fully sympathize with us in both the trials and the triumphs of the workplace.

Let me ask you, Christian, if you are fortunate enough to have employment, what is your reputation in your place of work? Is Christianity made attractive to others by your life, industry and witness there? There will be times when we are not popular at work because our God is not popular. Sometimes that is unavoidable. But what of your integrity and application in the workplace? If your reputation is not good, then you need to repent before God our Saviour.

Not long ago I happened to pick up a brochure produced by a little company for its staff. It was entitled *Make everyone a VIP*. It struck me that much of what it was saying was so close to the Christian principles of behaviour at work, and the company could obviously see the benefits of its staff adopting such behaviour. Here are some quotations from it:

> All too often, we forget to remind co-workers or employees that they are important. That is unfortunate, because doing so makes them feel better about themselves and about their work. Here are a few hints to keep in mind... Start on the right foot. When you meet new people greet them with interest. Stand up for them. Make eye-contact with them... After you have met someone

drop them a handwritten note to say that you enjoyed meeting and working with them... When you are talking to someone, listen to their responses. Check on yourself. Listen to your tone of voice. Is it helpful? Imagine everyone is wearing a button that says, 'Make me feel important.'

Some of that might be a little excessive but we can all see the common-sense behind what it is saying. So much of that is Christian in its outlook. It is calling for courtesy, generosity, graciousness in our contacts with others at work, instead of the hard-bitten aggression which so often predominates in offices and factories. Here is an opportunity for the Christian to surprise people by building others up instead of knocking them down. You may find you are derided for such an approach, but you are no fool to walk the Christian path, and you can find strength to take the knocks in Christ. To strive to make the workplace a more pleasant, encouraging place can enhance the performance of a working group. It is that kind of positive, open, friendly, honest kindness which will commend Christ. As we catch the spirit of the commands Paul sets out for the first-century slaves, we are given a clear view of godliness in the workplace.

The task facing Christians to recapture the workplace for Christ today is immense. But it can be done.

As we leave these verses concerning slavery we are to remember another impossible situation which Christians were used by God to turn round. William Wilberforce (1759-1833) and his friends stood up to, and campaigned against, the slave trade of their day. In 1784 Wilberforce became MP for Yorkshire. His conversion to Christ gave him a dynamic to lead the campaign against slavery, something which he had abominated since the age of fourteen. From 1784 onwards he repeatedly moved parliamentary resolutions against the British slave trade. It was a campaign with much stacked against it. His notions were not welcome to many prominent people. There were vested interests which fought Wilberforce. To finish the slave trade was not economically advantageous. Nevertheless what Wilberforce was seeking to do was right, and that was the main thing. The suppression of the slave trade took nearly twenty years, with its formal abolition being passed in 1807. He then went on to press for a European agreement to prohibit the trade.

He used his charm, his tact, his eloquence. He prayed and protested. He has left us a great example of how the giants of injustice and ungodliness in commerce can be overthrown, and Christ can be victorious in the world of business.

1. See Appendix for further discussion on how this could work out in practice.

7.
The motivation for godliness

Please read Titus 2:11-15

Genuine Christian living requires a certain holiness and self-denial, mixed with a tender, generous heart towards others. These characteristics are not theoretical ideals. They are to find expression in the real world. Paul has described something of what these characteristics mean in practice as, in the first ten verses of Titus chapter 2, he has spelled out godliness for men and women and how it applies even among the slaves of his day.

The problem in the new churches on the island of Crete was that Christians were just not responding to this requirement. There was a gap between the truth of the gospel they professed and the way they were living. The gap was caused first by a basic selfishness and subjectivism which seemed to come more naturally than usual to the Cretan national character, and secondly by various forms of false teaching in Crete which were tailor-made to reinforce people's preoccupation with the 'me first' attitude to life.

As we approach the third millennium after Christ, we live similarly today in what has been called 'the Culture of Narcissus'. In Greek legend, Narcissus, the son of the river-god, was incredibly good-looking and was passionately loved by the nymph Echo. However, he spurned her love, having instead become infatuated with himself and his own reflection mirrored in the water. The consequence was that both he and Echo pined away in frustration over their unfulfilled devotion — hers to him and his to his own reflection, which would disappear immediately he touched it.

Narcissus is a fitting symbol of the idolatry of our culture. The predominant religion of our Western society is the worship of self and our society is locked into the same prison of fruitless frustration as Narcissus. In the 'me-centred' generation when we get what we want, we find it isn't actually enough. And it never is.

The gospel truth of the Lord Jesus Christ is meant to lead people out of that prison into the joyful self-forgetfulness of the love and grace of God. But why should Christians live loving, outgoing, self-denying, godly lives? That is a question we have touched on once or twice already, but Paul deals with it head-on in these verses.

Why should Christian men be temperate and patient? Why should Christian wives be kind and submissive to their husbands? Why should Christian slaves show their masters that they can be fully trusted? Here is the reason: **'For the grace of God that brings salvation has appeared to all men. It teaches us to say "No" to ungodliness and worldly passions, and to live self-controlled, upright and godly lives in this present age, while we wait for the blessed hope — the glorious appearing of our great God and Saviour, Jesus Christ, who gave himself for us to redeem us from all wickedness and to purify for himself a people that are his very own, eager to do what is good.'**

Note that word 'for' at the beginning of the verse. Paul is giving the reason for, and spelling out the logic behind, Christian living. The motivation for godliness is the grace of God. Paul regards the grace of God in these verses as a past fact with a present significance. God's grace has appeared to us, and God's grace educates us, and so motivates us.

God's grace appeared (2:11)

The term 'grace' can mean beauty or elegance. When it is used of God it refers particularly to his beautiful character which delights in generosity to the undeserving. In chapter 3:4 Paul expresses a parallel thought as he speaks of 'when the kindness and love of God our Saviour appeared'. Grace is the kindness and love of God.

Here is an illustration of grace from another author which I once came across which I find helpful.

A poor farmer went to see his bank manager. He said to the bank manager, 'I've got some good news and some bad news. Which do you want to hear first?' The banker replied that they had better get the bad news over with first. 'Well', said the farmer, 'I've had such a bad year that I can't pay the mortgage I owe you on my house.' The bank manager looked disgruntled. 'There's more,' said the farmer. 'I've had such a bad harvest that I can't repay any of the money I borrowed from you to buy new machinery either.' 'That's bad,' replied the banker. 'I'm afraid there's more,' said the farmer. 'Last year I also borrowed money from you to buy seeds and fertilizer and other things, and I've had such a bad time that I can't even repay that to you.' 'That's terrible!' replied the bank manager. 'You had better tell me the good news now.' 'Well, the good news', said the farmer, 'is that I still intend to do business with you.'[1]

Now if we reverse the subjects in that story, it actually represents some profound theology. God's grace is that despite our total spiritual bankruptcy before him because of our sin, he still wants to do business with us. God's heart of compassion and spontaneous mercy to us in our failure and

moral ugliness is such that he still loves mankind and desires
to provide for us in all our needs.

Of course, the grace of God has a long history. The apostle
Paul, as a Jew, could look back through the whole Old
Testament history from creation onwards and see how again
and again God had taken pity on rebellious and undeserving
people. In particular the Old Testament records God's rescue
of the nation of Israel from bondage in Egypt and his bringing
them into covenant relationship with himself as an act of
God's pure grace. Just before he died, Moses spelt it out to
Israel in the book of Deuteronomy. He explained that it was
not because they were a large nation, or a morally superior
people, or an economically productive community that God
chose them (Deut. 7:7-8; 8:17-18; 9:4-6). They were none of
these things. In fact Israel was a nation who deserved destruction many times over. But still God chose them, rescued them
and loved them. He sent them prophets to guide them. He sent
judges to save them and kings to shepherd them. He chastised
them when they went astray. He encouraged them as they
followed him. God's grace has a long history.

Yet in verse 11 Paul speaks of the grace of God appearing,
being made visible, or materializing: **'The grace of God that
brings salvation has appeared.'** What Paul is saying is that
God's gracious dealings with Israel are like a shadow compared to the fulness of grace which has been ushered in with
the coming of the Lord Jesus Christ. In the Old Testament
times God dealt with his people at a distance, as it were. He
sent men as his agents. He gave them kings, priests and
prophets. He loved them from heaven. But now God our
Saviour has come himself in the person of Jesus Christ (2:10).
And now that he has come himself the fulness of his grace has
been made manifest in the salvation which he has brought.
Many times in the Old Testament God had saved his people.
But those rescues are only scale models of the true salvation
that has come in Christ. He rescued Abraham and Sarah from

their barrenness and reproductive deadness, but in Christ he has rescued us from death itself. He rescued the Israelites from slavery to Pharaoh in Egypt, but in Christ he has rescued us from sin, and brought us from the power of Satan to God. He brought Israel to a new land flowing with milk and honey, but in Christ he is bringing us to an eternal world, a new heavens and a new earth, the home of righteousness. The salvation which the Old Testament stories can only picture for us has come as a wonderful reality in the incarnation, death and resurrection of the Lord Jesus Christ. A new era of the world has begun in history. God has found full expression for his grace and has intervened directly to bring eternal salvation. His grace has appeared.

What is more, his grace is not restricted. It **'has appeared to all men'** (2:11). It is a historical fact accessible to all. Christ lived and died and rose again. It is preached and proclaimed and offered to the whole wide world. It is held out and made available to everyone in the Lord Jesus Christ. What is recorded of the life of Jesus in the Gospels often underlines this fact. Think of the lepers, outcasts of society. Think of the demonized man who lived among the tombs, and everyone avoided through fear. Think of the avaricious little cheat of a tax-collector, Zaccheus, whom everyone despised. Yet Jesus went out of his way to find these people and receive them and bring salvation to them. The grace of God reaches out to all. It reaches to 'Mary' the prostitute and Mary the virgin. It reaches to the fisherman Peter and the Pharisee Paul. Whoever you are, God loves you and has sent his Son so that whoever believes will not perish but have everlasting life.

Paul cannot think of salvation apart from the grace of God. It is the grace of God that brings salvation, not our achievements or deserving. It is all undeserved and unconditional, as we come to Christ. That is precisely why it is a salvation which can be offered freely to sinners and freely to all, because it is without qualification — it is salvation by grace. This cannot be stressed enough. The offer of salvation is real. God is no deceiver. He is the God who does not lie (1:2). 'The grace of God that brings salvation has appeared to all men.' This is the message which unlocks the prison of subjectivism and self, as Paul next goes on to explain.

God's grace educates (2:12-14)

The past fact of grace has a present continuing influence: **'It teaches us to say "No" to ungodliness and worldly passions, and to live self-controlled, upright and godly lives in this present age...'** The grace of God is here almost personified as a schoolmaster with the task of educating us in the art of living. The word 'teach' here indicates a total training. Our teacher firstly gives us a double denial. We are made to see why we must reject both ungodliness (practical atheism) and worldly passions (selfish desires rooted solely in this present age). Then our teacher secondly makes clear to us why we are to pursue self-controlled, upright and godly lives. This trio of virtues can be seen as covering all the relationships of our lives. Self-control refers to our relationship to ourselves and our behaviour. Uprightness refers to loving honesty in all our dealings with other people. Godliness refers to a humble, reverent and obedient walk with God who is at the centre of our lives. The grace of God is our schoolmaster to educate and train us in the art of living this way. How does the grace of God in Christ do that? Three avenues of spiritual education are suggested by verses 12-14.

1. Our heads (2:12)

First of all, grace changes our way of thinking. It educates our minds, giving us the reason for living godly lives.

Grace teaches us to abhor sin. The cross of Christ was necessary to deal with our sin. The cross teaches us that sin is no light matter. The Lord Jesus is God's eternal Son. God is holy and his antipathy to sin is such that unpardoned sinners must go to hell; and sinners are only pardoned as the price for sin was paid. And that price had to be nothing less than the substitutionary death of God's own sinless Son. The cross is the grand proof of God's righteous and ferocious antipathy to sin and therefore we must not fool ourselves into thinking that sin does not matter. God wants us to be at total war with sin in our personal lives. The grace of God in the cross of Christ teaches us the need for holy living.

One of the most dangerous threats to the life of the church down the centuries has been the error of antinomianism. This error is the idea that because Christ has atoned for sin, it does not matter if our minds are lax, or our discipline is slack as Christians, because Christ has paid for it all. But though Christ's atonement for sin is complete and thorough on our behalf, that is to draw the wrong conclusion from the cross. Imagine a father and son trapped in a remote cave, with an anti-personnel explosive mine positioned at the only exit. They are lost. The father checks this device and realizes that it is impossible to defuse it. They are trapped. Time goes on but there is no way out. They are certain to die of starvation if nothing else. Imagine that eventually the father, having with tears explained the situation to his loving son, decides that the only way to save his son's life is to go and throw himself on the mine in order that his son may go free. If the father carried out such a rescue, and his son escaped to freedom and to life, how would the son feel about anti-personnel mines for the rest of his life? Would he be likely to treasure them? Would he keep one on his mantelpiece as a point of interest in the home? No! He would hate the wretched device which killed the father he loved. Just so, though we are free, sin is the explosive which cannot be defused, and Jesus is the one who graciously sacrificed him-self to set us free. The grace of God in the gospel teaches us to hate sin. It teaches us to say 'No' to worldly passions.

Grace gives the rationale for love. If atheism is true, and the universe is simply about blind impersonal evolution, then all of life is just a chance event, and love has no ultimate call on us over any other way of living. In fact the attitude of survival of the fittest and 'looking after number one' would seem to make the most sense, certainly not self-sacrificial living for the good of others. But the fact that God's grace has appeared in Christ changes all that. It means that God is there, and God does care. He cared so much that in the person of Jesus he came and laid down his life for us. The cross demonstrates that God is love — real love that sacrifices itself, and gives itself for others, even for the unlovely and undeserving. That being the case, it makes sense for us to similarly live a life of love. Why? Because God is like that; then when we live a life of love, we are in tune therefore with ultimate reality, with God himself. To live selfishly, by contrast, is to be at odds with ultimate reality. We know deep in our beings that love is the right way to live, but atheism provides no basis for true love. In fact no other religion provides such a basis, for only Christianity tells us of a God who truly loves us, coming to live alongside us and suffer to rescue us. The grace of God, therefore, educates us and gives us the rationale for love rather than selfishness. It teaches us to say 'No' to ungodliness and 'Yes' to Christlike living.

But a full education for life includes more than the training of our minds. There is more to human personality than simply our thinking.

2. *Our hopes* (2:13)

God's grace educates our aspirations, for we live in a new context in Christ. We pursue **'godly lives in this present age,**

while we wait for the blessed hope — the glorious appearing of our great God and Saviour, Jesus Christ...'

As we have already been reminded, our faith 'rests on the hope of eternal life'. The Christian is someone who is waiting. Self-control, which underlies all godliness, involves the postponing of immediate gratification in the light of a more distant but greater goal. Unbelievers say to themselves that this life is all there is, and therefore give themselves over to their particular form of hedonism. 'Life is too short to be good,' is their philosophy. It was the philosophy of the aggressive sensualism which generally characterized the unconverted people of Crete in Paul's day, too.

But the Christian is someone who waits. He sees the present in the light of a better future. He spurns the so-called pleasures of sin in this present transitory world, in order to follow Christ, and so gain the far greater and eternal pleasure of the world to come. John Hooper was a godly bishop of the Church of England who was martyred for his biblical Protestantism in February 1555, during the reign of Mary Tudor. He was brought back to his diocese of Gloucester to be burned at the stake. As he approached the city a friend who cared greatly for the bishop tried to remonstrate with him, encouraging him to try to save his life by renouncing his faith. He urged the bishop to remember that 'Life is sweet, and death is bitter.' But to this the noble John Hooper returned the memorable reply that 'Eternal life is more sweet, and eternal death is more bitter,' and so he went on to seal his devotion to Christ by his martyrdom.

The Christian is someone who looks beyond this life, and ultimately to 'the blessed hope — the glorious appearing of our great God and Saviour Jesus Christ...'

The 'blessed hope' signifies the certain future prospect which brings blessing. The 'glorious appearing' is literally 'the appearance of the glory of the great God...' The Christian lives between the times. Not only has the grace of God appeared in Christ, but the glory of God will appear in Christ's return. God's glory is a glory which transforms those who see it. We are reminded that as Moses was allowed to see something of God's glory on the mountain, his own face shone (Exod. 34:29). Elsewhere in the New Testament, Paul reminds us that 'We, who with unveiled faces all contemplate the Lord's glory, are being transformed into his likeness with ever-increasing glory, which comes from the Lord, who is the Spirit' (2 Cor. 3:18). The blessed hope of the Christian is that when Christ returns at his second coming his glory will be unveiled, and there will be a quantum leap of transformation and eternal blessing for all his people, and for the whole universe. Then Christ, who is the firstfruits of the resurrection harvest, will transform the present, frail body of the Christian believer to be 'like his glorious body' (Phil. 3:21). The dead will be raised to eternal life. This final, open revelation of God's glory will bring a transformation cosmic in scope, and include freedom from all sin for the believer and the liberation of the entire subhuman creation from futility and corruption (Rom. 8:19-21).

Here is how grace educates our hopes and makes us content to shun sin and follow Christ, because of the prospect of God's glory before us. Note that here Paul affirms that Christ is God. We wait for 'the glorious appearing of our great God and Saviour, Jesus Christ'. The coming of God's glory is the coming of Christ. God cannot be separated from his glory; God and his glory are one; he shares it with no other. What began with the appearance of God's grace, salvation and a new way of life is brought to completion in the appearance of God's glory, as Christ returns.

The lesson here is that the presence of Christ is a transforming presence with the ultimate transformation coming at his return. But already, by his Spirit, we can know something of the presence of Christ for our lives, to transform us. One incident which underlines this is the aftermath of the terrorist attack in 1993 on the St James's Church in Capetown, South Africa, which made international news. This is what Frank Retief, the minister of that church, has written about those events:

> One night a group of gunmen burst into our church. They sprayed the congregation with gunfire and hurled hand grenades into the crowded pews. It was part of the campaign of terror waged by certain groups in the run-up to the first democratic elections in South Africa. When the dust settled, eleven people lay dead and more than fifty were injured, some maimed for life.
>
> In the aftermath of this dreadful act, we as a congregation experienced the truth of the Lord Jesus Christ, our shepherd. We did indeed experience his peace, in the midst of pain, shock and suffering. Even though our grief was very deep, we found that we did not have to revise anything we had believed concerning him. We found ourselves experiencing one of the great privileges of being a Christian — having his presence in an almost tangible way, even when the way for us was very dark. And that is exactly what you too can expect.[2]

So there is a definite sense in which this hope, although in the future, can be experienced to some extent now. There is a peace which the Spirit of Christ can bring, which will deliver us from responding wrongly, even when we are sorely provoked, and will give us a foretaste of the future glory which will impart self-control amid immediate temptations. The grace of God encourages us to look beyond this life and enables us to experience something of Christ's presence now, and so educates our hopes and trains us in godliness.

3. Our hearts (2:14)

A full foundation for Christian character addresses not just our minds and our aspirations, but our feelings and emotions as well. Our hearts are touched as Paul explains that Jesus Christ is the one **'who gave himself for us to redeem us from all wickedness and to purify for himself a people that are his very own, eager to do what is good'**.

Notice the purpose behind what in God's grace Christ did for us. It was to rescue us from wickedness, and to make us his special people marked out by the fact that we are eagerly pursuing doing good in our lives. This is Christ's purpose, so not to live his way is to be out of step with Christ. Once again we see how God's grace is educating us in a godly way of life.

Paul uses two metaphors here to explain what Christ has done for his people. He gave himself 'to redeem' us and 'to purify' us.

The first metaphor would make first-century readers like Titus think of the slave-market. To redeem someone was to pay a sum for the slave's release, or to bring the person into one's own service. Either way of looking at it is suited to what Christ has done by his death for the believer. With his blood he paid for our sins and so set us free from sin's dominion and consequences and has brought us into his own service, which is true freedom.

The second metaphor is that of washing and cleansing. Through the cross Christ has released his Spirit into the lives and hearts of his people. We are given new life. In Titus 3:5 Paul speaks of 'the washing of rebirth'. In Ephesians 5:26 he speaks of 'the washing with water through the word'. Clearly as he speaks of rebirth, and the word, Paul has in mind an inward purifying of our hearts which flows out of the work of Christ. The grace of God, then, affects our inner lives. And surely included in this is a new love and affection for Jesus Christ which expels our former preoccupation with self and sin, and makes us zealous to please him out of thanks for all he has done for us.

Paul tells us that Jesus 'gave himself for us', or in our place. Back in 1987 two RAF crewmen died when their F111 crashed on exercise in New South Wales, Australia. It seems that the plane was going to crash into the town of Tenterfield. If the pilot and navigator had ejected immediately they were in trouble the plane would have smashed into the town, killing many people. But the airmen delayed their ejecting to steer it away out into the desert. The local newspaper editor said, 'There's a feeling in our town that we owe our lives to those two. It would have been no trouble for them to eject.'[3] Wickedness had taken hold of us and God's wrath was heading for us and would have crashed down on us because of our sin. But Christ took the controls and steered the war-plane of God's judgement away from us, giving us life, and suffered the consequences himself instead. He did it to rescue us from wickedness and to make us his own. We are to let that sink in. He died for us. When it does sink in, it touches our hearts. His love for us moves us to love him. God's grace educates our hearts. It touches our affections.

This is so important for true godly living. If one vast threat to the life of the church throughout history has been moral laxity and antinomianism, the other great threat is the opposite danger of legalism. The legalist is the person who has an outwardly respectable life, and keeps all the rules, but it is all an empty façade. God addressed the legalist as he spoke through Isaiah the prophet and said, 'These people come near to me with their mouth, and honour me with their lips, but their hearts are far from me' (Isa. 29:13). Without a sincere love for God, the legalist is a person who draws his satisfaction from his performance in comparison with others, rather than from the fact that God loves him. This was the case with the Pharisees of Jesus' day, who made a great outward show of religion and loved the applause of men. They were outwardly

strict and starchy about their rules and observances but in-
wardly their hearts were hard and unfeeling towards both
people and God. The bottom line of legalism is that it has never
grasped the grace of God. Legalism at root is about trusting our
own religious activity, rather than trusting in the mercy of
God. It is based on our abilities to achieve rather than God's
ability to be merciful. That being the case, it is self-absorbed
and in a way self-centred. It can never set people free into the
self-forgetfulness of love and true service. The whole direction of God's grace is to lead us, not only away from moral
laxity, but also away from the deadness of legalism. The grace
of God shouts loud and clear that God loves us freely. This stirs
our affections. We love him because he first loved us. He has
a place in his heart for sinners and we are to respond to him
from our hearts. God is a God of grace. Our acceptance with
him is not dependent on how 'good' we have been or how
'spiritual' we feel. It is all of his free mercy. We are not to rely
on our own efforts, neither are we to fall into antinomian
laxity. Rather we are to live a life of thankful love.

We will honour God's law, for Christ died to satisfy the
law's demands for our sins. But we will not be hollow legalists,
for Christ died for us because he loved us. We will approach
God's commands from the direction of love, not of legalism.
God's grace educates us away from laxity and legalism into
the self-forgetful love of God and his service. So the gospel of
God's grace gives us a thorough education of head, hope and
heart. Our whole inner life is trained to follow Christ. This is
the motivation for godliness.

What to teach (2:15)

Here we have reached the end of a definite section of Paul's
letter. The opening verse of the chapter was like a literary

opening of the bracket, and verse 15 is the equivalent closing of the bracket. Paul had explained to Titus: 'You must teach what is in accord with sound doctrine' (2:1). He has opened up the requirements for behaviour which matches the gospel for men and women, old and young, and for slaves. Thus he has explained how the gospel motivates us in living according to that gospel lifestyle, touching our minds and our hearts. Now Paul rounds off and underlines what he has explained by saying, **'These, then, are the things you should teach.'**

They must be declared and spoken out. He will go on to explain to Titus something of how he should teach these things, but we will leave looking at that until the next chapter.

The most important thing to realize is that it works. The teaching of the biblical gospel does transform people's lives, leading them away from sin and self-centredness to godliness.

The story of the mutiny on the *Bounty* has often been told, but it is worth reminding ourselves that the full story provides a wonderful witness to the transforming power of the gospel.

In 1787 Captain Bligh had left Tahiti, an island paradise in the Pacific, and was sailing home to England with his crew. But one morning he woke to find himself facing a mutiny. The crew had little back in England to look forward to and they were bewitched with the sin and leisure of the Pacific islands. The officers were cut adrift in a small boat, while the rest of the crew, under Fletcher Christian, sailed back to Tahiti. There they persuaded some of the women to come with them. They set out again from the island. They had no plans but at last came to the unknown island of Pitcairn. This island seemed like another earthly paradise. They took all they could from the ship and set it on fire and sunk it, so that no passing ship would know they were there. Then they let loose all their passions. They were free to do whatever they wished. But, of course, because the human heart is sinful, it turned into ten years of virtual hell. They began to make alcohol from the plants that grew there. Men spent days, even weeks, completely drunk. Soon fighting and killing broke out. They became like animals in their behaviour. One man went mad and jumped over a cliff. Ungodliness reigned.

Eventually there were only two of the mutineers left. One man was named Edward Young and the other Alexander Smith. Edward Young was quite elderly, and he became ill. But these two persisted in their wayward behaviour, so much so that one night the women and children seized the guns and barricaded themselves off in a particular part of the island. They did not want any more from these men.

One day Young found the old ship's Bible from the *Bounty*. Smith couldn't read and, strangely, in one of their more sober moments, Young began to teach him to read from the Bible. They started to learn, reading the Bible through from Genesis. They saw that God is holy, and that they were sinners. They were somehow gripped. Their reading of the Bible began to affect them. They realized their lives were an offence to God and began to change. It took time to read. The children on the island noticed the change first. Not too long afterwards Young died. But Smith read on (by now he had learned to read for himself), and he came to the New Testament. Something remarkable happened to him as he read of Jesus. This is what he wrote of his experience: 'I had been working like a mole for years and suddenly it was as if the doors flew wide open and I saw the light, and I met God and the burden of my sin rolled away and I found new life.'

From that moment on everything on Pitcairn Island changed. Smith began to read the Scriptures to the women and children. Interestingly enough, eighteen years after the original mutiny (1805) a ship from Boston came across Pitcairn Island. The captain came ashore. There he found a community of people who were godly. They had a love and peace about them which the captain had never seen before. When he got back to Boston he reported that in all his travels he had never met a people who were so good and gracious.

It worked! The grace of God had educated them. It had redeemed them from wickedness and made them into a people eager to do good. The truth had led to godliness. What the gospel did there, it is able by God's grace to do anywhere.

1. This story is taken from David Seamans, *Healing Grace,* Scripture Press, 1989.
2. Frank Retief, *From Tragedy to Triumph,* Word Books.
3. This story is told in Graham Twelftree, *Drive Home the Point,* Monarch Publications, 1994.

8.
A different kind of freedom

Please read Titus 2:15 - 3:2

'They are complete idiots, aren't they? They are totally uninformed and out of touch with reality. They make me so angry! They ought to be sacked. They have about as much sensitivity as a man who eats a pork pie at a funeral! Trumped up little Napoleons with brains the size of a pea! They are intolerant, utterly unprofessional, completely incompetent!'

Who is being spoken about here? It is a parody, of course, but I think a fairly truthful parody of how many people react to anyone in a position of authority who doesn't see things their way. That kind of aggressive, abusive spirit is often encountered today. Sometimes it goes under the pseudonym of self-assertiveness, and 'standing up for my rights', but frequently there is far more venom and slander in it than that.

We start here, because although on the surface they touch on a variety of subjects, actually our verses in this section are focused around a Christian's response to other people, especially those in authority. Paul tells Titus, **'These, then, are the things you should teach. Encourage and rebuke with all authority. Do not let anyone despise you. Remind the people to be subject to rulers and authorities, to be obedient, to be ready to do whatever is good, to slander no one, to be peaceable and considerate, and to show true humility towards all men.'**

'Authority' is a dirty word in our modern world. It is seen as the antithesis of personal freedom. It stops us doing what we want to do. It stands in our way. It was a dirty word too in first-century Crete, where Titus had been sent to straighten out the churches recently planted there. As we have now noted on a number of occasions, the Cretan national character had sadly degenerated to that of a devious idle yob, a self-absorbed bully (1:12). It was not very beautiful, and such a selfish character (even if it is disguised beneath a veneer of charm) is never more starkly exposed than when it comes into collision with legitimate authority. It wants to have its own way and if it cannot have it, it will become abusive and bitter and sometimes violent.

Tragically, we see civil violence ever increasing in our world. How often it is these days that protests by various pressure groups and single-issue organizations are aggressive, abusive and frequently result in violence against the police who are seeking to keep order. Concerns for personal freedom today seem to go hand in hand with a hostile spirit.

Unfortunately, some of the newly converted people on Crete had changed little since they had become Christians. As yet, their unconverted attitudes still clung to them in many areas of life and a bellicose outlook towards authority was one such area. So, as Paul has explained to Titus what he is to teach these people in the churches, he is aware that Titus will probably meet opposition and have his own authority challenged by such characters. That is how this subject of authority and a Christian's response to it comes on to Paul's agenda.

This issue is no mere sideline. It is not simply something of curiosity value. It is an issue of serious pastoral application to the churches today. For many Christians, the greatest hindrance to their spiritual effectiveness, and the reason why they do not grow as Christians, is due to bitterness or anger of some kind. In Paul's letter to the Ephesians the command not to

grieve the Holy Spirit is followed immediately by the command to 'Get rid of all bitterness, rage and anger ... along with
every form of malice' (Eph. 4:30-31). A bitter outlook grieves
the Holy Spirit and so stunts our spiritual development. Very
often such bitterness in people goes back to their attitude to
someone in a position of legitimate authority who has crossed
them. It may be a church leader, a parent, a hospital doctor, a
teacher at school, a supervisor at work, or even the national
government. We may be upset by the political party in power
and their perceived injustices and allow ourselves to go
beyond the limits of legitimate displeasure and be kept in an
ongoing state of resentment and discontent. This will damage
us spiritually if we are not careful. The Lord calls us to love,
even those with whom we disagree.

Some Christians have been upset by church leaders in the
past. The church leaders' actions may or may not have been
wise and proper. However, this is allowed to produce such an
antipathy towards those in church leadership generally that
these Christians from then on will never join a church and
come under the authority of any oversight, no matter how
godly. Often such Christians wander from church to church,
never settling, and never pulling their weight in the family of
God. This does damage to the church and damage to the individual. Nurturing resentment and anger, we become people
with an attitude problem, sour and bitter rather than the
beautiful people God would have us be.

We shall consider this subject of our response to authority
by looking at these verses under two headings.

An attitude to be rejected (2:15)

**'These, then, are the things you should teach. Encourage
and rebuke with all authority. Do not let anyone despise
you.'** The type of authority in view here is the spiritual

authority of a Christian teacher. His authority does not lie in himself, but in the fact that he has been called and gifted by God to teach the Word of the Lord. As Paul's delegate Titus shared the apostle's authority. Similarly, as the Christian teacher is called and gifted to teach the Scriptures, then as he is true to the Word of God, his ministry comes with the authority of the Word of God. His teaching is not a bundle of hints and suggestions he thinks might be helpful, but the word of the Lord to the people. This, then, is his authority. The attitude to be rejected is therefore that of despising the teacher of the Word.

Despising a Christian teacher can occur in all kinds of ways. Moses was despised by the Israelites because the road on which he led them was uncomfortable and tough. The people of Nazareth regarded the Lord Jesus with contempt because his teaching disturbed their racial prejudices and they were so familiar with him (Luke 4:23-29). The intellectuals at Mars Hill in Athens despised Paul's preaching of Christ, because they felt it was too simplistic for them. The charismatic 'super-apostles' who were seeking to settle in the church in Corinth despised Paul because they felt their miraculous powers made them superior to the insignificant little Jew who always seemed to be ill or in trouble of one sort or another (2 Corinthians). Paul knew that some people would take the opportunity to despise Timothy and his ministry simply because he was younger than they were. Perhaps his youth affronted their self-importance, or showed up their own lack of spiritual progress as older people (1 Tim. 4:12).

Despising a Christian leader can come in different degrees. It can look down upon him with contempt as if he were worthless ('Why doesn't he do a proper day's work?'). Or the word used here in Titus 2:15 means simply to ignore him. Some Christians despise their teachers simply by always having some reason for getting round what they say ('It's only his interpretation, his opinion, so we don't need to take any notice').

But whatever the trigger, or the degree of despising, the underlying reason is always the same: 'To listen to him is beneath me.' It is pride. But pride is a spiritual killer because it is the devil's character (1 Tim. 3:6) and God resists the proud but gives grace to the humble (1 Peter 5:5).

What is most interesting to consider is the fact that if anyone had proper reason to despise and look down on spiritual leaders, it was the Lord Jesus. After all, he is the Son of God, and he came to a religious system that was corrupt and had had its day and was about to be swept aside. But you never find him despising religious leaders. He opposed their hypocrisy wherever he found it, but he did not despise what they stood for. He told the lepers he had cleansed to 'Go and show yourselves to the priests, as the law says.' To Peter he indicates that he is the one for whom the temple in Jerusalem was built, 'Yet it is still right for us to pay the temple tax.' We know it was the custom of Jesus to be found in the synagogue on the Sabbath. There is no despising of legitimate religious authority here, but rather a wonderful humility in God's Son.

There are things, of course, which Christian leaders ought to do to help people have the right attitude towards them. Here I am not talking of a false and manufactured show of authority. I can remember one friend who attended Bible College in the 1960s telling me that he was told at college that he must always wear a suit. Whenever any of his flock met him, whether it be in the church or at home at breakfast time, he must wear a suit, for this would always give him an air of authority. Well, that is a false authority. The Christian leader's authority cannot be put on like a theatrical costume. It has to be an authority with integrity.

Here in our verse, the apostle Paul gives us the clue as to how to help people have a right respect for Christian leaders. Leaders help people not to despise them when four things are true.

1. They are to teach the apostle's doctrine

Paul, as the apostle of Christ, spells out to Titus: 'These, then, are the things you should teach.' Because the only authority teachers have comes from the Word of God in the power of the Spirit, they too must allow the apostle to set their teaching agenda. They are to teach, not their own ideas, but the Scriptures, being fully aware that as they do so they have all the authority of God behind them, for Jesus said, 'Heaven and earth will pass away, but my words will never pass away' (Luke 21:33).

2. They are to teach in a way which encourages people

Some people are rebels against God's Word, but many Christians never rise to obey God's Word, not because they are rebellious, but because they are disheartened and weak. A Christian teacher will lose his authority with such people if all he ever does is to lash their consciences with thunderbolts from the pulpit. They will feel that the teacher is uncaring and insensitive and has no understanding of their situation. The pastor must show such people that he loves them as he brings the Word of God to them. So it is that Scripture is full of God's love and promises and 'Do not fear's. People will respect and respond to a man who they realize truly feels for them and seeks to put new heart into them.

3. They are to be brave enough to rebuke the people when they need it

As we have previously noted, the great temptation for the Christian teacher is to be a people-pleaser. He must be sensitive to the needs of people, but never fall into the trap of being frightened of them. Some people fail to obey because they are weak, but others fail to obey through pure rebellion. The only way to do good to such folk is to give them a stern warning and rebuke. 'Faithful are the wounds of a friend,' says the book of Proverbs, and the only way to truly love such people is to oppose them to their face. A Christian leader can lose his credibility with people if he is too frightened to do this. He must do it with a calm spirit, and from a motive of love. But he must do it.

4. *Underlying all these things there must be sincerity and integrity*

Paul has already pointed this out to Titus in chapter 2:7-8. Sincerity will mean that not only is the leader teaching God's Word to other people, but he is also applying it to his own life. Integrity will mean a diligence in making sure he has understood God's Word rightly, and also a humility to admit when he has got things wrong.

These principles of how to teach will help people not to despise their teachers. In a day when it is fashionable to despise those in authority they will enable people to respect their leaders and, more importantly, to respect the Word of God.

In closing this section I need to ask you, Christian, a question. What is your attitude to the leaders of your congregation? You are not to idolize them. But you are to respect them. Is your attitude to them helpful to you and to them? Do you pray for your leaders? Consider what Paul has said in these verses. Think it over.

Moving away from the negative, Paul's comments now go on to direct us positively concerning the Christian attitude to legitimate authority.

An attitude to be fostered (3:1-2)

Having raised the subject of authority in the church, Paul moves on to a different kind of authority: **'Remind the people to be subject to rulers and authorities, to be obedient, to be ready to do whatever is good, to slander no one, to be peaceable and considerate, and to show true humility towards all men.'** The type of authority primarily in view here is that of the civil authority and law of the land.

As we have seen, the Cretans were known for their truculence and aggression as well as their self-centredness. At one time the island had been a haven for pirates. Certainly the general attitude was one which did not think very highly of the idea of submitting to the law. And so as Paul has this matter of our attitude to those in authority in his mind he is keen to make sure that Titus teaches the Cretan Christians not to be trouble-makers, nor the cause of civil unrest, but to adopt a different outlook on life: 'Remind the people to be subject to rulers...' They must leave their old attitudes behind. Once again it is worth looking at the relationship of the Lord Jesus Christ to the civil authorities of his day. We should remind ourselves that Jesus was not a political revolutionary. He had no political aspirations as far as this world was concerned. After he had performed the miracle of feeding the 5,000, the people were keen to make him king by force (John 6:15). He had the power of God and the popular support of the masses. The door was wide open for him to take up government. But John's Gospel tells us that Jesus' reaction was instead to go and hide himself. Christ was more concerned to work within the constraints of the existing political system than to lead a coup against it, even if it was corrupt. He exercised the right to be critical of those in authority, but believed that God's Word is mightier than the sword. His kingdom is not of this world. He did not deny Caesar his taxes (Mark 12:14-17). He taught his followers to carry the baggage of the soldiers of the occupying Roman forces the second mile (Matt. 5:41). He took seriously his own teaching of loving his enemies, and praying for persecutors. So it is that Paul writes that Titus must 'remind the people to be subject to rulers...'

Christians are not to cut themselves off from society or civil life, but are to participate as loyal citizens wherever possible. In this way they are to be 'obedient'. Not only so, but they are to be on the lookout to 'do good', and so take every opportunity of being a blessing to society.

This attitude of willing submission to authorities for the good of society is based on an attitude of service towards all mankind. So the Christian's responsibility towards all people comes into view in verse 2. Christians are to be taught 'to slander no one, to be peaceable and considerate, and to show true humility towards all men'. This is not the confrontational self-assertiveness of today.

This is not 'doormat' Christianity, or just letting people walk all over you. It is not passive but active. But it is active with love, not aggression. The Christian is to be involved in positively confronting evil with good. We are not to be slanderers. It is very easy to speak badly, expressing dark suspicions without evidence, about various officials or the government of the day. This is sometimes the bread and butter of the secular media in our day. But it is not for the Christian. We are to be taken up with seeking positive good for others, whether they be those in power or not.

Paul desires Christians to be peaceable: that is, we are to be those who consciously resist taking violent actions in difficult situations in order to preserve relationships. We are to be considerate. Consideration is that forethought which bridles personal concerns in order to make room for the concerns of others. Paul desires Christians to be humble (or meek). That meekness is a balanced estimate of ourselves and our status before the Almighty God who has saved us by grace, which enables us to serve others and work for their good. This is Christlikeness. This is beautiful.

A fully rounded Christian character, then, is very different from the ugly, aggressive, abusive spirit which has come into vogue in our day. It lays down its rights for the good of others. It is humble, not proud. It seeks not confrontation, but peace wherever possible.

A different kind of freedom

We are caused to wonder what underlies this different way of life. What stimulates this Christlike, humble attitude to authority and to other people? In particular, we must ask, what makes this a credible alternative to the resentment and aggression which colour so much of the world's response to authority?

The long answer is all the things which are found in 3:3-8 to which we will pay attention in the next chapter. But the short answer to these questions is a different kind of freedom from that of the world.

For a godless world, authority and 'other people' are a threat to liberty. They are a threat to that 'do as I like' view of freedom. We cannot park our car wherever we like because of the traffic wardens. We cannot play our music at full volume, because of the neighbours. Our responsibilities to other people in our families impinge on our time. This is why present society finds authority and responsibility so irksome. It is also why the rebel is a hero in our popular culture. But this is not the way Paul has outlined for us. It is not the way for the Christian who has truly understood what we have in Christ. In Christ there is a totally different understanding and outworking of freedom, which is genuine liberty.

Authentic freedom, said Jesus, comes from knowing and obeying the truth (John 8:31-32). The truth is that this is God's world, not ours. We are not God; we are God's creatures, made to glorify and enjoy him as we are redeemed through Jesus Christ. Hence, true freedom comes as we put God, not self, at the centre of our lives, for then we are beginning to fulfil the role for which we are actually designed. As the world strives for its 'freedom' it has to continually strive to gain control over its circumstances, in order to be able to do as it wants. This is an ultimately impossible task. By contrast Christian freedom is an inner freedom of the heart blessed by the Holy Spirit, which transcends its circumstances. It is the freedom of being decisively committed to God who loves us. It is, then, the freedom of those who are not still wondering anxiously where their loyalties should lie, or where they are going. It is the freedom of dependency on God and no longer being dependent on our own failing and limited resources to cope with life, but of knowing the power of God in our lives to walk in his ways. Most importantly, it is the freedom of knowing we are forgiven, knowing ourselves to be children of God, knowing ourselves to be possessors of eternal life through the free grace of God. In a word it is the freedom of being able to 'do everything through [Christ] who gives me strength' (Phil. 4:13). So it is that a Christian can be both a servant and free at the same time.

A few years ago I remember going to London with my wife Ann to see the successful show *Les Misérables,* based on Victor Hugo's great novel of the same name. The story excited me very much because in many ways it spoke of the gospel of Christ. Set in France in the last century, it tells the tale of Jean Valjean. He has served a nineteen-year jail sentence of hard labour for stealing a loaf of bread and by the time he is released from prison he is a hardened, violent man, hating all authority. He has been released from prison, but he is still not free. He has to carry an identity card as an ex-convict, and as he travels no innkeeper will let a dangerous felon like him stay the night. He wanders for days until finally a kindly bishop takes him in.

But when the house is asleep Valjean gets up and steals the bishop's silver plates and makes off. The next morning three policemen knock at the bishop's door. They have found Jean Valjean escaping with the stolen silver and the law is ready to put him in chains for life. Jean has failed to live up to the freedom he had.

However, the bishop does the very opposite of what the police or Jean expect. He greets Jean like an old friend. 'I am delighted to see you,' he says. 'Have you forgotten I gave you the candlesticks as well? They are worth a good 200 francs. Did you forget them?' Jean's eyes widen in disbelief. The bishop answers the police that the silver was a gift to Jean and, satisfied, they eventually leave. The bishop's kindness does not change when they are alone. He gives Jean the silver and says, 'Do not forget that you promised me to use the money to make yourself an honest man.'

The next day as Jean travels on from the bishop's house his knee buckles under him. It is as if he is overwhelmed by an invisible power and the weight of a bad conscience. He falls to the ground exhausted. 'What a wretch I am!' he cries. Then his emotions overflow, he bursts into tears of remorse, guilt and shame. But then those tears turn into tears of broken-hearted love as a great sense of God's love and having been totally forgiven sweeps over him. It is like an extraordinary light that completely transforms his life. The bitterness of his soul is melted, and now he is truly a free man! He is free to love, ready to do good to all. The story unfolds as a vengeful detective, who dislikes Valjean, stalks him for the next twenty years trying to prove something against him. But he cannot catch him out, for Valjean is a changed man.

Valjean has been transformed by the knowledge of full forgiveness. That same forgiveness in all its fulness is ours as we come in repentance and faith to the Lord Jesus who died for sinners. That same freedom, in all its fulness, is there for us.

9.
The basis for godliness

Please read Titus 3:3-8

Fairly frequently, my wife and I take pre-marriage Bible studies with newly engaged Christian couples as they come to tie the knot. Not long ago as we went through the study with one couple, it dawned with great force on the young man just what the New Testament requires a good husband to be as a loving, Christlike head of his family. His reaction was: 'I honestly don't know whether I am up to it. The standard is too high.' It was a frank response, and I am sure that many of us have had the same feeling as we have been challenged by the Scriptures in the various areas of our lives.

Jesus calls us to be holy, to deny self, to love even our enemies, let alone our wives. He means Christians to be different. As we have noted already, in chapter 4, sometimes it is such demands which keep people back from committing themselves to Christ. 'I know that what is being said is right,' they think, 'but I could never keep it up. I would just be a hypocrite. So it's not worth trying.'

I think Paul was expecting the Cretan Christians, whom Titus had been sent to help, to have a similar reaction to the demands of godliness. For example, he had written, as we saw in the last chapter, that the people must be 'subject to rulers and authorities ... obedient ... ready to do whatever is good ... peaceable and considerate ... to show true humility towards all men'. 'It's too hard,' they might say. So it is that Paul's concern in the verses we are now to consider is to tell Christians why they can be different. He spells out the basis on which a godly life is possible.

He has already dealt with the motives for godly living in 2:11-14, but here he explains the foundation and resources which make a godly life possible. He has dealt with the 'why', but here he gives us the 'how'. He is telling us the gap between what we practise and what we preach is not an impossible gulf to bridge. There is a solid basis for genuine Christianity.

The two necessary ingredients are a genuine salvation (3:3-7) and our genuine response (3:8).

A genuine salvation (3:3 -7)

Here is the basis of a godly life: **'At one time we too were foolish, disobedient, deceived and enslaved by all kinds of passions and pleasures. We lived in malice and envy, being hated and hating one another. But when the kindness and love of God our Saviour appeared, he saved us, not because of righteous things we had done, but because of his mercy. He saved us through the washing of rebirth and renewal by the Holy Spirit, whom he poured out on us generously through Jesus Christ our Saviour, so that, having been justified by his grace, we might become heirs having the hope of eternal life.'**

The reason why it is possible to live differently is because a fundamental change, or transition, has occurred in the history of the world. 'At one time...' (3:3) leads into 'But when...' (3:4). Paul is not speaking of our personal transformation by conversion to Christ so much as the new era of God's dealings with the world which has been opened up through the incarnation, death, resurrection and ascension of the Lord Jesus. Christ's coming has changed everything.

Sometimes changes do occur in history which make what was once impossible become possible. Sir Frank Whittle invented the jet engine in the earlier decades of this century. For the first time things became possible which were not possible before, such as supersonic flight. With the invention of liquid fuel rockets it has become possible to do what was impossible before — to put a man on the moon. And in a similar way the coming of Jesus has made a new way of life possible for ordinary men and women, boys and girls.

We can picture what has been done through Jesus as God building a bridge between two ways of life. The two ways of life are found in our verses. The old way of life is referred to in verse 3: 'At one time we too were foolish, disobedient, deceived...' The new way of life is found in verse 7: 'Having been justified by his grace ... having the hope of eternal life.' The intervening verses tell us about the bridge from one to the other. This bridge is genuine salvation.

1. The old life (3:3)

'At one time we too were foolish, disobedient, deceived and enslaved by all kinds of passions and pleasures. We lived in malice and envy, being hated and hating one another.' That is how the world is without Christ. That sums up the history of humanity without the Spirit of God. That is how we all are, left to ourselves.

Our minds are foolish and deceived, because we only ever see things from our own self-centred point of view. So we are disobedient. Remember, as an example of this, how we contrasted Paul's requirement of obedience to authorities with the aggressive, slanderous attitudes which often pre-dominate towards authority. In particular, as we are foolish, our minds are disobedient and rebellious to God's laws and deceived into thinking that it does not matter and there will be no consequences.

Our wills are enslaved by passions and pleasures (3:3). There are habits and temptations in our lives which we cannot break out of, even though our consciences tell us they are wrong. They keep us bound. The story is told that in Belgium in the fourteenth century a very fat man was kept in a prison with no lock and no door. Walled up, he was too big to squeeze through the open entrance. All his jailer did was to send him delicious fattening food which he couldn't resist eating. Instead of dieting so he could escape, he got fatter and fatter. He was a prisoner of his own appetite. We are like that. We are hooked on self and pleasure (even the strange pleasure of nurturing resentment) and refusing to give it up.

Our relationships are those which beneath a veneer of respectability are based on malice and envy. Society is a place of 'dog eating dog'. Paul describes it as 'being hated, and hating one another'. Think of the shallowness of human relationships in your place of work. Think of the behind-the-back comments which break out when someone is given promotion, while others are passed over. Paul is not wrong in his assessment of godless society.

We can control the power of the atom, but we cannot control passion and envy and malicious tongues. We can keep a little baby alive outside the womb by marvellous technology, but we cannot keep God's commandments. This is the old life. We see it all around us.

But it is possible to be different, for God has built a bridge to a new life in Jesus Christ.

2. The bridge (3:4-6)

The bridge to new life is all of God's construction. Paul tells us it was God's mercy, brought about for God's motives, and issuing in God's method of changing our lives.

God's mercy saves us. Faced with human selfishness and sin, what did God do? **'But when the kindness and love of**

God our Saviour appeared, he saved us...' He saved us. He sent his only Son, the Lord Jesus Christ, the epitome and the fountain of God's kindness and love to us, to take our sins and deal with them at Calvary.

In a previous chapter we used the story of the RAF pilots who steered their plane, which was crashing, away from the town of Tenterfield in New South Wales and in doing so gave up the chance to eject and so lost their own lives. That is a fitting picture to us of God's rescue of us from our sins. The town did not save itself. It was none of the townspeople's doing. The pilots, and the pilots alone, saved the town. In the same way, our sins were taking us to the destination of eternal hell, but God intervened. It was God's move and God's mercy. Jesus came and saved us; single-handedly, without any help from us, he dealt once and for all with our sin and its consequences and set our lives on a totally new basis. By his atoning death in our place, all our sins, past, present and future, are paid for. We are right with God. We are fully forgiven.

God's motive for rescuing us is referred to next. What was God's reason for rescuing us? Paul tells us in verse 5: **'He saved us, not because of righteous things we had done, but because of his mercy.'** We were not rescued because we deserved it. But God's motive for doing it was pure love, pure philanthropy, pure mercy. This mercy of God is equivalent to his faithful covenant loving-kindness. It is dependent on his unshakeable faithfulness alone, and on nothing else. This is the origin of our salvation in Christ.

Sometimes we meet people who say something like this: 'Oh, I would like to be forgiven, but I don't deserve it. I'm not good enough.' Though we all understand such talk, in fact it is stupid. It is like saying, 'I'm too dirty to have a bath,' or 'I'm too smelly to have a shower.' Our sins, our lack of deserving, are the very things Christ died to deal with. So how can they be obstacles to forgiveness? Of course sinners like us do not deserve forgiveness, but that is what forgiveness (over against a bargain or settlement) is all about. It is about *undeserved* mercy. 'Righteous things we have done' are not only not good enough, they do not even enter into the equation.

Here is where the gospel is such good news for sinners. It precisely fits our case. Our consciences tell us that, in truth, we have nothing to commend ourselves to God. But the good news of Christ is that we need nothing. It is this free mercy which melts the hardened hearts of sinners. Caught up in the spider's web of sin, we sinners are not only agents but also victims of sinful acts. So many people live hurt and pitiful lives, and their sins are partly a blind and foolish searching after love and comfort in life. Consider the woman Jesus met at the well who had been married to five husbands and at the time Jesus spoke to her was living with another man. We can imagine her going from one man to the next with the thought that 'Perhaps this one will really love me and cherish me.' Sinners are lost souls in search of love. How marvellous the gospel is, as it speaks of the mighty and free love of God given to us in Christ though we are so undeserving! How wonderful is God's grace!

What is *God's method* of changing our lives? This makes the third element of Paul's marvellous exposition of salvation. To be forgiven is one thing, but how can our lives be changed? This is the crux of the question Paul is seeking to answer in these verses. How can we be saved not just from the guilt and consequences of sin, but from the power of sin over us? Here is what Paul explains to us: **'He saved us through the washing of rebirth and renewal by the Holy Spirit, whom he poured out on us generously through Jesus Christ our Saviour'** (3:5-6). His method of changing us is the gift of his Holy Spirit. By his Spirit he begins a work of renovation in us reaching to the very roots of our personalities. Paul uses three phrases for the Spirit's activity.

The Christian has been *washed*. This is Paul's overall description of what has happened to the inner life of a Christian. The washing referred to here is inward, because it is a washing 'by the Holy Spirit' (not water as in baptism). It seems that behind Paul's words here he has in mind the Old Testament promise of the gift of the Spirit given through Ezekiel. God promised his rebellious people, using the symbolism of ceremonial washing: 'I will sprinkle clean water on you, and you will be clean; I will cleanse you from all your impurities and from all your idols. I will give you a new heart and put a new spirit in you; I will remove from you your heart of stone and give you a heart of flesh. And I will put my Spirit in you and move you to follow my decrees and be careful to keep my laws' (Ezek. 36:25-27). This Old Testament prediction of the blessing of the Spirit which the Messiah would bring in the new covenant is the experience and the privilege of the Christian. The three ideas of sprinkling, a new heart and a new spirit seem to co-ordinate well with the three terms Paul uses in Titus of washing, rebirth and renewal.

The washing which the Spirit brings is accordingly primarily a moral and spiritual cleansing. Ezekiel spoke of being cleansed from impurities and idolatry. Here is the basis of a changed life.

The Christian has also been *reborn* (3:5). A new life has been planted within us. It is not simply earthly life; it is life from heaven. The powerful Holy Spirit has taken up residence in us. God is no longer simply God above — the Father; or even God with us — the Lord Jesus; but God *in* us — the Holy Spirit. These three persons of the Trinity are of course mysteriously one. We do not become 'God', or even 'a god', as the fallacious New Age teaching would encourage us to believe. But the Holy Spirit, as Comforter, Counsellor and powerful Friend, resides in us.

The Christian has also been *renewed* (3:5) by the Holy Spirit. This term is almost synonymous with rebirth but highlights a different aspect. Rebirth emphasizes change, renewal vitality. When the Holy Spirit enters a person's life, he comes to make us more truly human, to make us more what we really ought to be. This is renewal. He begins to remove the old damaged characteristics and replaces them with new ones. Ezekiel speaks of the old heart of stone, hard and indifferent to God's commands, being removed, and a new heart of flesh, soft and sensitive to God's Word, being put in its place.

This is how God leads us from the old life into a new way of living. This is the basis for a changed life. By God's Spirit we are given new purity, new power and new responsiveness to God and his ways.

Paul's emphasis in verse 6 is on the abundance of the gift of the Holy Spirit God has given. The Holy Spirit is the one **'whom he poured out on us generously through Jesus Christ our Saviour'**. Christ's ascension into heaven was followed by the pouring out of the Spirit on the church at Pentecost. Paul has spoken of the kindness and love of God appearing and a new era of world history having begun. In particular through Christ, the Holy Spirit has been given and made ever available in all the fulness of his power and resources through faith in the Lord Jesus Christ.

Note that these verses tell us that there is no salvation without the reception of the Spirit: **'He saved us through the washing ... by the Holy Spirit.'** Conversely when someone comes to faith in Christ, there is the work of the Holy Spirit. As Ezekiel said, his work cleanses people from idols, not least the idol of self, and brings them to submission to God.

You might be saying to yourself, 'Oh, it's impossible for me to change!' But throughout the whole Bible God tells us that it is impossible situations which the Holy Spirit is best at dealing with. How can the whole of creation spring into being out of nothingness? It is impossible. Yet by the Spirit's power our world and the whole wide universe came to be. How can an old and barren couple of nearly 100 years old have a child?

It is impossible. Yet by God's power Abraham and Sarah had a son, Isaac. How can one man strike down 1,000 in battle against him? But Samson did, by the Spirit of God upon him. How can a young teenager possibly overcome a seasoned warrior who stands over eight feet high? But David overthrew and killed the giant Goliath because the Spirit of God was upon him. And the great news of the gospel is that because of what Christ accomplished at Calvary, not only have our sins been forgiven, but the Spirit of God has been poured out and made available to all who believe. The wonderful Holy Spirit is no longer, as in Old Testament times, restricted to a few prophets and kings and heroes and heroines; he is available to us all. How can a narrow-hearted, bigoted, murderous, self-opinionated man like Saul of Tarsus ever be different? But by the Spirit of God he was made different. He became the loving, warm-hearted, preacher of truth, the apostle Paul. He is the very writer of this letter to Titus. If God could renovate Saul by the power of his Spirit he can renovate anyone.

3. The new life (3:7)

The result of God's saving work is that the Christian has been reborn by the Spirit. That rebirth means that something has already happened to the Christian and also points to something which is to happen in the future. We have been reborn of the Spirit, **'so that, having been justified by his grace, we might become heirs having the hope of eternal life'**.

The Christian has been justified; that is, we have a new status of being totally forgiven and counted as righteous in God's sight. We have also become heirs. We have been accepted as children in God's family. We have a new relationship therefore with God as our Father. Because of this we are able to look forward with certainty to the fulness of heaven and eternal life.

When we take stock we realize we have a new heart, a new power, a new desire, a new status, a new relationship and a new future. All this adds up to a new life and the ability to be different from the world. This does not mean we shall be perfect in this life. We have not arrived in heaven yet. But it does mean that we have the resources to fight against sin, and make progress, and be different from the world. We have the resources to change. Closing the gap between what we believe and how we behave is really possible.

As Paul has emphasized here, the power and activity of the Holy Spirit, enabling us to deny self, take up the cross, and follow Christ in the way we live, are crucial. I love this little story from the Scotland of former days which illustrates our need to be continually prayerful and to walk closely with the Spirit in order to know victory in the Christian life.

A farmer in Kilmarnock was once engaged in threshing corn. He had been busy all day and there was a considerable heap on the floor as a result of his labours. But when he came back to his corn the next day all the threshed corn was gone. This occurred a second and a third time, till the farmer could bear it no longer. So he resolved to watch all night as well as work all day. He had not been waiting long when the thief appeared and began to gather up corn. Leaping upon him the farmer tried to put him down, so that he might either bind him or hold him until help arrived. But the thief proved stronger than he and laid the farmer on his back and had almost strangled him when a friend suddenly arrived and came to the farmer's rescue.

Having hold of the thief after the farmer was on his legs again, the friend said to him, 'What will be done to the thief?' 'Oh, bind him,' was the answer, 'and give him to me on my back, and I will set off with him at once to the prison at Tain.' His friend did as he requested, and off set the farmer with his burden. But as he went out of sight of his friend, in a hollow of the road, the thief succeeded in breaking the cords that bound him and fell upon the farmer, giving him a rougher time than before. The farmer would have been killed had not his friend come up in time to save him. His friend again asked what he would do now. The answer was the same as before, only he added, 'I will be more careful this time.' So again he started with his troublesome burden on his back and all was quiet until he came to a dark part of the road, through the woods at Calrossie, when the fastenings were again broken and the farmer maltreated worse than before. Once again his friend came to his help, but now the farmer would not part with his friend until he had accompanied him with his load to the prison. His request was granted, the jail reached, the thief locked up, and the farmer, forgetting his friend in the delight at getting rid of his tormentor, with a light step set out for his home.

Just as he had banished all fear from his heart, and was indulging in anticipation of peace for the future, in a moment the thief, who had escaped from his cell and hurried to overtake him, sprang upon him from behind and, with even more than his former fury, threw the poor farmer to the ground and now would have killed him outright, had not the wanted help of his friend once more come in time of need. Once more his friend asked, what would be done. The farmer, worried and wearied, cast himself at his friend's feet and seizing him with both hands cried, 'Let the day never dawn on which you and I shall for a moment be parted, for without you I can do nothing.'[1]

So it is that in the person of the Holy Spirit we have a powerful Friend, by whom we can overcome our temptations and sins and be different. He dwells in us, never to be parted from us. Without him we can do nothing, but with him we can do all things, as we prayerfully co-operate with him.

These, then, are all the resources. Self-centredness can be defeated. The gap between our belief and our behaviour is not an impossible gap to close. It is all there for us in the genuine salvation which God has provided for us in all its completeness in the Lord Jesus Christ.

But if we are not yet Christians, how do we experience his salvation personally? How does it become ours? And if we are Christians, how do we continue in it and use its resources for our lives? The next verse gives us the answer.

A genuine response (3:8)

'This is a trustworthy saying. And I want you to stress these things, so that those who have trusted in God may be careful to devote themselves to doing what is good. These things are excellent and profitable for everyone.' Referring to what he has just spelt out about salvation and what God has done for us in the Lord Jesus Christ, Paul says, 'This is a trustworthy saying.' That not only indicates that the previous verses may have been a well-known confession of faith among early Christians, but also immediately gives us the clue to the response God requires from us. God does not lie. His gospel is trustworthy. So what? So we should trust. We should trust the Lord and his promises and put ourselves in his hands. That this is the response God requires is underlined by the way Paul describes Christians in verse 8. He describes them as 'those who have trusted in God'.

Let us reflect on three things about genuine trust in the Lord.

1. There are two kinds of men in an army

There are those who follow their captain reluctantly, out of mere duty. 'Oh well, there is nothing else for it, so I had better follow.' That is not the kind of trust meant here. There are others who follow with confident expectation. They trust in their captain and his abilities to do the job and get them through their mission. It is that kind of trust which is biblical faith in Jesus. It is that confident conviction which the good news seeks to evoke in us towards the Lord Jesus Christ. He truly loves us. We know that because he went to Calvary. He has power to bring us through anything. We know that because he rose from the dead and now is enthroned in heaven. We can really trust him. We can follow him expectantly and confidently. That is the response to Christ which brings genuine salvation to us personally.

2. *Such trust is active, not passive*

We do not simply sit back and view God's salvation as an audience might view a play. Rather we get up out of our seats and become actors in God's drama. Those who have trusted in God must be 'careful to devote themselves to doing what is good' (3:8). With our trust in Christ we begin to attempt to do things we could not do before and, by the power of Christ, we find to our amazement that we can do them.

At Jesus' command Peter could step out of the boat, and walk on the water as he kept his eyes fixed on the Lord! Trusting in the kindness and power of Christ's word, the man with the withered arm found he could do what he had never been able to do before — stretch out his arm, and as he did so it was made whole.

At Christ's command, relying on him as our Captain, we seek to be good husbands and loving wives, and we find we can be. At Christ's command, trusting in him we attempt to witness to others for the gospel, and we find we do meet with some success. At Christ's command, looking to him in faith, we try to forgive our enemies, and help the needy, and overcome sin in our lives, and we find we can make progress. Our trust in Christ is not passive but active.

3. It is the gospel which evokes faith in Christ from us

The preaching and stressing of the things of the gospel, says Paul, are 'excellent and profitable for everyone' (3:8). Whether you are a Christian or not a Christian, the same message of God's salvation is what you need. It can inspire faith in Jesus for the first time and so bring eternal salvation. It can encourage the weary Christian and keep us going in the faith. It is profitable for everyone.

Sincere faith, trust in God through Jesus Christ, is the required response which brings all the realities of genuine salvation into our lives.

Paul's purpose

Now, looking back over this section, can you see what Paul has done? We started by thinking about people saying that Christian standards are too high. We started by thinking about people who say, 'I would become a Christian, but, no thanks, because I couldn't keep it up.' And do you see what Paul has done in what he has spelled out here? He has lovingly knocked from under us all our excuses. All we sinners need is available.

You can be different for God, for God can make you different. Christian, God is able to enable you to close the gap between what you believe and how you behave. Non-Christian, there is actually no legitimate reason for you not to become a Christian, and respond positively to Jesus. Trust him. Trust him wholly. Trust him now.

Do not put it off. Let me ask you something, if you are not a Christian. When you have had your lunch or evening meal, what do you do with the leftovers? How would you like to be given the scraps to eat, the leftovers of someone else's dinner? Of course you would not. But if you are saying to God, 'I will become a Christian, but later; not now,' then what you are really saying is, 'God, when the devil has taken what he wants from the plate of my life, you can have the leftovers.' That is what is actually happening when you refuse to respond to the gospel right away. You would not want other people's left-overs. You may well refuse them. And God does not promise to accept you any other time but now. Now is the day of salvation. He promises to receive you now. Come to Christ, if you are not a Christian. Come now. Trust him and follow him in genuine response to his genuine offer of salvation.

1. This story is taken, in a slightly edited form, from *The Days of the Fathers in Rossshire,* published by Christian Focus Publications.

10.
Devoted to doing good

Please read Titus 3:9-15

Titus was left on the island of Crete by Paul to straighten out the error and self-centredness in the newly planted churches there. As we come to the closing section of the letter from Paul to Titus we see that the thrust of his parting emphasis is contained in verse 14: **'Our people must learn to devote themselves to doing what is good, in order that they may provide for daily necessities and not live unproductive lives.'**

This matter of 'doing good' has been a recurring theme running throughout the book. Let us just follow the thread of 'doing good' in Titus for a moment. An elder, we were told, must be someone 'who loves what is good' (1:8). By contrast Paul condemns the false teachers as 'unfit for doing anything good' (1:16). The elder women were to be encouraged 'to teach what is good' (2:3). Titus himself was to set an example to the young men 'by doing what is good' (2:7). Paul expresses the purpose of Jesus' death on the cross as being 'to redeem us from all wickedness and purify for himself a people that are his very own, eager to do what is good' (2:14). In outlining the Christian's attitude to authority and to other people Paul has commanded that they 'be ready to do whatever is good' (3:1). In our last chapter we saw that the gospel is to be emphasized by Titus 'so that those who have trusted in God may be careful to devote themselves to doing what is good' (3:8). Finally, we have come now to the last section and we have this parting emphasis of Paul: 'Our people must learn to devote themselves to doing what is good' (3:14).

This emphasis shows another aspect of the burden of the whole letter concerning closing the gap between what Christians profess to believe and how they practically behave. Closing the gap is not simply a matter of saying 'No' to temptation, but of positively pursuing that which is intrinsically noble and beneficial. It is a matter of breaking out of self-centredness into generous and godly service. As we shall see, Paul uses two different words for 'good' in Titus. Between them they cover a spectrum of meanings, from the moral sense of that which is pure and wholesome, through to that which is beneficial and beautiful because it is well suited to the circumstances and is honourable and ethically right. The ideas of 'good' in the sense of being spiritually profitable and productive come to the fore in this last section. The good news must lead to good lives. A little child once prayed, 'Lord, make the bad people good, and the good people kind.' This is so crucial to the credibility of the church before the watching world, and so important for the integrity of the church before the eyes of God, that Paul feels he cannot close the letter without impressing on Titus once more that Christians must 'devote themselves to doing what is good'.

We shall gather up his motive in these final verses under two main headings.

Profitable and unprofitable teaching (3:9-11)

In the last chapter we saw that in 3:8 Paul says that the truth and the doctrines of the gospel are 'excellent and profitable'. Here in verse 9, he evaluates the false teaching as 'unprofitable': 'But avoid foolish controversies and genealogies and arguments and quarrels about the law, because these are unprofitable and useless.' The concerns and preaching of the false teachers do not lead to Christlike character and good works, but just to selfishness, division and controversy. Here is an echo of the words of the Lord Jesus concerning false prophets: 'By their fruit you will recognize them. Do people pick grapes from thornbushes, or figs from thistles? Likewise every good tree bears good fruit, but a bad tree bears bad fruit. A good tree cannot bear bad fruit, and a bad tree cannot bear good fruit' (Matt. 7:16-18). So with the theme of the good news leading to good lives in his mind, Paul contrasts the profitability of the gospel with the unprofitability of the false teaching. We shall note three things here.

1. Paul's assumption

Paul assumes that it is the teaching, the doctrine, the world-view which we are taught and accept which is the key in shaping our behaviour. It is, as he declared in the very first verse of the book, the truth received into our hearts which will lead to godliness of life. It is error or lack of teaching in our hearts which will lead to complacent, lax Christianity and a decadent society.

Now, of course, many people today deny that connection. For example, people say, 'It is perfectly possible to be a decent, moral person and to be an atheist.' While that may be true of certain idiosyncratic individuals who, in fact, are still living under the subconscious influence of their Christian heritage, generally speaking the Bible would dispute that. Psalm 14:1 tells us that 'The fool says in his heart, "There is no God,"' and goes on to explain in the same verse that the inevitable consequence is that 'They are corrupt, their deeds are vile.' Without God, sinful self is unleashed to do as it pleases. Paul explains to us in the first chapter of Romans that when people turn from God, then morals in society go in one direction, and one direction only — downhill. We do not just have Scripture's word for this; we can see it in history. Look at what has happened in the Western world over this last century as man decided that he had come of age and no longer needed the God and the Christianity of his forefathers. We now live in a society awash with the pollution of sin, filth, violence and corruption, with all the consequent tragedies of broken families, poverty, depression and increasing fear. There is a connection between what people are taught and the way they live. As a man thinks in his heart, so is he.

The tragedy is that the modern church no longer sees this connection. Instead it sees the answer to its current ills purely in terms of the power of the Holy Spirit.

Actually the ills of the church come from a rather different direction. They come in part from the fact that we live in a culture which has murdered and buried the idea of absolute truth. Everything is relative and a matter of personal opinion in the eyes of the world. So it is that ideas and teachings can only be held in a very provisional, loose way and there is therefore no urgency to work them out in practical living. Modern relativism cuts the connection Paul makes between truth and life, between teaching and action. This same attitude has rubbed off onto the church. Progress in holy living, victory over temptations and changes of habit are now sought in terms of special prayer and a new anointing of the Spirit, rather than thorough teaching. Problems are seen in terms of a 'spirit' which needs to be cast out of a Christian (where do you ever find such a thing in the New Testament?) or an unlocking of the emotions through special prayer. Meanwhile, teaching and personal Bible study are often despised and written off as just 'head knowledge' or 'just the preacher's interpretation'.

Certainly, preachers must be careful to exegete Scripture correctly and apply it to the heart, but this whole attitude of downplaying the role of sound teaching is completely foreign to the New Testament.

The modern church has followed its own version of the world's line of cutting the connection between truth and life. But according to Jesus it is the truth which changes people's lives. He prays for his disciples to his Father, 'Sanctify them by the truth; your word is truth' (John 17:16). To the Roman church Paul explains that Christians are 'transformed by the renewing of your mind' (Rom. 12:2), not by experiences which downplay or bypass the mind, or put it into 'neutral'. In this very letter to Titus we have been studying he began by stressing that it is 'the truth that leads to godliness' (1:1).

Coloured by the subjective, feeling-orientated atmosphere of our times to an extent much greater than it realizes, the modern church has pursued excitement and emotion to the neglect of truth and teaching. We have cut the connection which Paul has spelled out.

While we do indeed need the Spirit's power he is also the Spirit of truth. He is the Spirit who inspired the Scriptures and witnesses to the gospel. He is the Spirit who brings a certainty and conviction so that we do not hold Christian teaching loosely or lightly. He is the Spirit who brings assurance, so that we know the truth, and know that we know it, and are therefore concerned to live it out, and to share it with others.

A church which emphasizes experience of the Spirit while decrying the need for sound doctrine is not approaching problems from Paul's direction. Always in the New Testament Paul is concerned for purity of teaching, for he knows that the control room of a human being is ultimately the mind, and it is only good teaching firmly based on the eternal truth of God that will lead to good lives.

2. What makes teaching profitable or unprofitable?

Secondly, let us ask the question, what makes the teaching of the gospel 'profitable' and the false teaching 'unprofitable' so far as transforming people's lives for the better is concerned?

Paul gives us very little to go on in Titus as to precisely what the false teachers on Crete were declaring. Understandably he is concerned to set forth the truth, not the error. But their teaching involved **'foolish controversies and genealogies and arguments and quarrels about the law'** (3:9). The false teachers seemed to have some novel way of approaching and interpreting the Old Testament law, which resulted in many arguments and quarrels. They seemed to focus on Old Testament family lines, and rituals of the law. We ought immediately to be suspicious of people who overemphasize the Old Testament. Not that the Old Testament is anything other than the very Word of God. But the Old Testament, by its own witness, is preparatory and points towards the coming of Christ. The Lord Jesus is the central figure in God's great work of redemption. So we best understand the Old Testament in the light of the New Testament and the word of Christ displayed there.

We can only surmise the precise details of the false teaching, but its emphasis on the law and genealogies leads us in the direction of thinking that it stressed people's natural abilities (passed on in the family?) and the achievement of some form of religious standard to live up to either by virtual effort or supposed personal enlightenment. But all such teaching is useless for two reasons.

Firstly, *it is based on a naïve view of human nature*. It sets an ethical or ritual standard and teaches that we must strive to achieve and so gain acceptance. But it forgets the fact and power of sin in our lives. It is the truth of the total fallenness of human nature which frequently underlies any erroneous teachings simply because such a truth is naturally unpopular to proud human nature. While sin does not make us as evil as we possibly could be, it taints every part of us and vitiates all possibility of salvation through personal achievement of whatever kind. Such teaching, which fails to take sin seriously, is doomed to failure.

In the 1920s a man named Frank Buchman started the Oxford Group later renamed Moral Rearmament. He emphasized four absolutes for living. These were absolute honesty, absolute purity, absolute unselfishness and absolute love. Relativism had not then totally taken over. The movement made a deep impact at the time and challenged many people to undertake a personal moral pilgrimage. It taught that you did not need Christian theology, or the old-fashioned gospel; you simply must strive for goodness. But where is that movement now? What lasting impression has it left on the life of our nation? None. Such movements, even those full of splendid good intentions, inevitably fail. They cannot be sustained. Human frailty, because of sin, is too great. They neither recognize the power of sin, nor have an answer to it. Ultimately therefore they are unprofitable.

The second reason why such movements fail is because *they do not preach the Lord Jesus revealed to us in Scripture.* It is not only the moralistic movements that focus on personal effort which fail here, but also the movements that stress personal enlightenment. Such teachings encourage their followers to look within themselves instead of looking away from themselves to the living Saviour, who died for our sins and rose again. Instead of emphasizing the historical, once-for-all atoning work of Jesus, they major on seeking personal spiritual experiences and altered states of consciousness. The Quakers, a movement started by George Fox in the seventeenth century, were a group which began with what may well have been a true touch of God's Spirit. But soon they started to emphasize looking inward rather than looking to Jesus. These movements tend to see our greatest need as that of enlightenment from our spiritual ignorance, rather than forgiveness for our sinful guilt before God.

George Whitefield, the great eighteenth-century evangelist, comments on the Quakers in a couple of places in his journals. During a return voyage to America he writes,

'Expounded with power in the morning to the sailors, and lent my cabin to the Quaker preacher in the afternoon. He spoke with much earnestness, but in my opinion his foundation was wrong. He seemed to make the light of conscience and the Holy Spirit, one and the same thing, and represented Christ within, and not Christ without, as the foundation of our faith; whereas the outward righteousness of Jesus Christ imputed to us, I believe, is the sole fountain and cause of all the inward communications which we receive from the Spirit of God. Oh, that all of that persuasion were convinced of this; till they are, they cannot preach the truth as it is in Jesus.' As Bible Christians we too value the felt sense of Christ in our hearts as precious and wonderful, and to be sought diligently. But even that is not to take priority over Christ's objective atoning work dealing with our sin.

While he was in Philadelphia, Whitefield again wrote in his journals, 'Went in the evening to the Quakers' meeting and felt somewhat in sympathy with the man that spoke. But I heartily wish they would talk of an outward as well as an inward Christ; for otherwise we make our own holiness and not the righteousness of Jesus Christ the cause of our being accepted by God. From such doctrine may I always turn away.'

We remember that it was men like Whitefield, not the Quakers, who so preached as to be used by God to revive the church and to transform the moral face of both Britain and America in the eighteenth century. It is the biblical gospel of Christ crucified redeeming us from sin which only is truly profitable. What makes the gospel profitable is its radical and realistic teaching about human sin, and the good news of the atonement for sin completed once and for all by the Lord Jesus Christ at Calvary. The gospel therefore is more than just a teaching; it leads us to a person — to Christ and to God himself. It leads us away from ourselves and to him who loves us and is alive for evermore.

The Western world faces a rising crime rate in our day. Back in 1770 William Romaine, the great preacher of London, published a tract entitled *A Method for Preventing the Frequency of Robberies and Murders*. In it he argues that although the law of the land and the penalties of the courts are useful, all they can do is to contain crime. He maintains that the actual problem lies in the sinful condition of humanity and therefore the only true solution lies in the transformation of human nature — in other words, Christian conversion. Therefore, he concludes that the government should support and finance the preaching of the gospel! He is saying the same as Paul. It is the gospel which is profitable. Everything except the truth of Christ in the gospel is useless.

3. Why Paul adopted this attitude to false teachers

So, thirdly, we can understand why Paul takes the attitude he does to false teachers in 3:10-11: **'Warn a divisive person once, and then warn him a second time. After that, have nothing to do with him. You may be sure that such a man is warped and sinful; he is self-condemned.'**

The false teachers' errors were troubling the churches and causing controversy and division. Paul refuses to enter into dialogue with these heretics. Rather than talk theology with divisive persons he tells Titus to give them one warning, then give them a second chance if they do not repent at the first. After that they are to be rejected. Paul here seems to have in mind the procedure of church discipline instituted by the Lord Jesus Christ: 'If your brother sins against you, go and show him his fault, just between the two of you. If he listens to you, you have won your brother over. But if he will not listen, take one or two others along, so that "every matter may be established by the testimony of two or three witnesses". If he refuses to listen to them, tell it to the church; and if he refuses to listen even to the church, treat him as you would a pagan or a tax collector' (Matt. 18:15-17).

The Lord Jesus speaks of three warnings, while Paul speaks of only two. The discrepancy is probably that the Lord's first warning is a private warning, and Paul simply concentrates on the two public warnings with witnesses and with the church. Refusal to hear the publicly endorsed apostolic word is tantamount to passing judgement on oneself. He who refuses to listen is hard-faced and resistant. 'You may be sure that such a man is warped and sinful,' so do not be diffident in taking the sad but necessary action. By refusing the apostolic truth and clinging to error, 'He is self-condemned.'

Turning this argument around for a moment, often in cases of church discipline we ask, 'What is the mark that someone is repentant?' The answer is: 'a willingness to hear, receive and positively respond to the Word of God'. We cannot gauge the depth of remorse in anyone's heart, nor are we called to do that. Only God knows people's hearts. All we can ascertain is how they respond to the Word of God. Are they willing to obey? Do they show that by their actions? If the answer is 'Yes', then that is good enough, for church discipline is not aimed at being punitive, or at getting 'justice', but at reclaiming the offender.

So the profitable teaching is the biblical gospel. The good news leads to good lives. Our ethics are rooted in the gospel and in conversion by the gospel to Christ. What about you? Have you found Christ and been spiritually reborn? If not, seek Jesus by humility, repentance and prayer until you find him. You must. This is where to begin. But if we have found Christ, how are we to go on? This leads us to consider the final verses of the letter to Titus.

Productive and unproductive lives (3:12-15)

'As soon as I send Artemas or Tychicus to you, do your best to come to me at Nicopolis, because I have decided to winter there. Do everything you can to help Zenas the lawyer and Apollos on their way and see they have every-thing they need. Our people must learn to devote them-selves to doing what is good, in order that they may provide for daily necessities and not live unproductive lives.'

It may well be that Paul's secretary, to whom he has been dictating the letter to Titus, has put down his pen and Paul himself writes these last few verses in his own hand as was his custom. This may explain the more personal references we find in these closing sentences too. But it is also here that he stresses the need for Christians to be those who are devoted to doing good. To be devoted means to have a single aim and to persevere in that aim no matter what. That is how Christians are to pursue the goal of doing good, for their God is a God of goodness, who in his goodness has saved them. They are not to live unfruitful, self-absorbed, unproductive lives. Rather they are to be fountains of goodness.

Let us ask a couple of questions.

1. What does Paul mean by a productive life?

We can answer that question in a general way from the whole letter first of all. Paul uses two different words in speaking about goodness in the letter to Titus. The first *(agathon)* means that which is intrinsically good and so beneficial to others. The second *(kalos)* refers to that which is intrinsically good, and so is beautiful to behold. Paul wants to see Christians living beautiful and beneficial lives.

In previous sections of the letters we have seen many different aspects of this. The elders are to be those who live blameless lives, with strong, warm, hospitable families, and who hold firmly to the Christian faith and by teaching and kindness love to do good to others. The older women are to lovingly inculcate a godly, loving lifestyle in the younger women by gentle and wise teaching and the sharing of years of experience. Doing good is, by kindness, teaching and example, to be beneficial to those around us materially, morally and spiritually. It is to live so that in every way we, in accordance with the gospel of grace and as we have opportunity, do all in our power to 'make the teaching about God our Saviour attractive' in all the relationships of our lives. We are to live beautiful, beneficial lives. We are to live lives which make a blessing for others and give honour to the name of Christ.

We can also answer the question about what makes for productive lives more particularly from these verses at the end of the letter. Our verse 14 makes it clear that a productive life is one which, given the opportunity to work, earns its own keep and provides for the needs of others, providing for **'daily necessities'**. To live by faith is not to seek to live without visible means of support (though sometimes God does miraculously provide for us). Rather, living by faith in Christ generally includes following Christ to the carpenter's bench or wherever our skills take us, to earn our living and provide for our dependents. This is down-to-earth doing good.

We can also see from verses 12 and 13 that being devoted to doing good also involves supporting the work of the gospel in whatever way we can. These verses were addressed to Titus. In verse 12 Titus is asked to come to Paul as soon as possible at Nicopolis, a seaport on the western coast of Greece. Then he asks Titus to do all he can to help Zenas and Apollos. Both these men seem to have been experts in the law and the Old Testament (Acts 18:24). Perhaps Paul had asked them to visit Crete to combat the false teachers by their knowledge of the

Old Testament which the false teachers were misusing. Whatever their precise task, they were men involved in gospel work
and as Paul asks Titus to **'see that they have everything they
need'** he is obviously wanting the Christians in Crete to get
involved with helping them. Thus this thought naturally runs
into verse 14, where the idea of all Christians pursuing doing
good is experienced. Christian folk do good as they do whatever is needed by way of prayer, hospitality, finance or other
support to help gospel workers. We do good when we give to
the poor and needy. But we also do good as we support the
spreading of gospel truth. We can do good by the sacrificial
giving of our money.

Now let us ask a second question. Having seen what a
productive Christian life is, let us ask about how such a life is
constructed.

2. How does a productive Christian life emerge?

Paul says, **'Our people must learn to devote themselves to
doing what is good.'** The two key words here are 'learn' and
'devote'.

Firstly, a productive Christian life emerges *by way of a
learning process.* By our conversion to Christ, by our new
birth, by our justification by God, a new life has been inaugu-
rated in us. It has begun, so we need to learn to live it out in
practice.

One of the most crucial parts of that learning process may
seem obvious, but is often missed or only partly understood by
us. Christians need to continually learn that the gospel applies
to them. The gospel is not just for non-Christians; it is for
Christians too. There is forgiveness for *our* sins, the sins *we*
have fallen into as Christians. Sometimes we adopt an attitude
which almost denies this. We have begun as Christians and
trusted Christ for forgiveness, but somehow think that, now

we are Christians, when we fall Christ cannot really forgive us and love us; after all, we have let him down so badly! It is true that we have let him down, but he still loves us and has forgiveness for us. There is forgiveness and love for religious people! We have to learn to be humble enough to realize that as Christians we need the same medicine every day. We have to learn that God is gracious enough that he loves us still, even when we have let him down as Christians. As we continue to learn this we grow in thankfulness to God, which is the heart of all true spirituality and true Christian service (Col. 2:6-7).

Also, of course, we have to learn to be productive, by learning what pleases God. When we come to Christ we are ignorant of God's ways. We need to learn from Scripture the Christian way of living, Christ's commands, God's wisdom. We need to learn to co-operate with the Holy Spirit, and to respond to God's Word. We need to train ourselves to be on the look-out to do good, in a way which is not threatening or overbearing, but sensitive to others. We need to learn to be people of prayer so that our service is in God's strength, not our own.

Secondly, a productive Christian life requires *devotion*. We have already handed out devotion and thanksgiving to the Lord because of his grace to us. But in verse 14 Paul is referring to being devoted, by way of our love to God, to doing good works. Devotion to one thing requires saying 'No' to other things. Devotion to good works will require being single-minded. If we are going to give more money to support missionaries, or help the needy, then we will have to spend less on ourselves. If a mature Christian woman is going to find time to befriend and encourage a younger woman in the church, then that time will have to be taken from somewhere else. Devotion means that priorities have to be set, and they have to be maintained. Frequently young people are prepared to get involved in some work for the church. Perhaps it is evangelistic work among children, or visiting the elderly. However, if a better offer comes up one week — it is someone's birthday party, or they have the chance to go out to the theatre — then they are missing from the activity. We must not be too legalistic about this, but it can mean that although they start in doing good, they show no consistency, no devotion. Truly productive Christian lives require devotion. Today there is much talk of evangelizing nations, and winning cities and towns for Christ. Those are fine ambitions. But so often we are looking for a quick fix. Back in the seventeenth century, the Puritan Richard Baxter won the town of Kidderminster to the Lord. Almost the whole town became believers, and there was worship not only in the church, but the vast majority of the homes in the town as Christian families prayed together. A town was won for God. But it was no quick process. It took Baxter years of praying, steady preaching and visiting house to house. A great impact was made. But it required devotion. It included battling on in the work even when he felt ill. It required sticking to one priority. Are you willing to let God set your priorities, for time, money and energy?

But devotion to doing good is not simply about stickability. It is not a grim determination. It flows from a heart of generosity and kindness. It is this spirit of love which Paul always seeks to stir up in Christians. It is this same spirit of tenderness and care which is reflected in the verses with which Paul closes his letter to Titus: **'Everyone with me sends you greetings. Greet those who love us in the faith. Grace be with you all.'** God's grace is with us, and it leads us to be gracious to others. To have God's grace with us means that not only are we forgiven, but we are God's children, with access to all the resources our Father can provide. So equipped, we can pursue the work of doing good with a generous heart and in a spirit of loving fellowship. It is salutary to realize that very soon life will be past, and we shall stand before God. We shall be asked how we have used our lives. Christ pictures the scene for us in his great parable of the sheep and the goats when 'the

Son of Man ... will sit on his throne in heavenly glory'. The King will say to some, 'Come, you who are blessed by my Father; take your inheritance, the kingdom prepared for you since the creation of the world. For I was hungry and you gave me something to eat, I was thirsty and you gave me something to drink, I was a stranger and you invited me in...' To others the King will say, 'Depart from me, you who are cursed, into the eternal fire prepared for the devil and his angels. For I was hungry and you gave me nothing to eat, I was thirsty and you gave me nothing to drink, I was a stranger and you did not invite me in...' The two groups ask, 'When did we do this, Lord?' The King's reply is: 'I tell you the truth, whatever you did for one of the least of these brothers of mine, you did for me.'

Here is the great urgency behind Paul's words: 'Our people must learn to devote themselves to doing what is good.' It is only as the good news of salvation by God's grace issues in good lives, forgetful of self and concerned for others, that we have genuinely received the gospel and been forgiven. We are not saved *by* good works, but we are saved *for* good works. Self-centredness must be defeated. The gap must be closed. Paul has reminded Titus that Jesus 'gave himself for us to redeem us from all wickedness and to purify for himself a people that are his very own, eager to do what is good' (2:14). On the last day Christ's people will be recognized by these good works which the gospel has wrought in their lives. In them it will be seen that it is indeed 'the truth that leads to godliness'.

11.
Straightening out the self-centred church

Having looked at all that Paul has written to Titus concerning what needs to be done to straighten out the churches in Crete, we now need to try briefly to put all the pieces of the jigsaw together in order to get a final overview.

The churches in Crete were churches with a gap. They were rebellious and prone to reject authority (1:10; 2:15; 3:1). They were influenced by false teaching which was subverting family life (1:11). They were not showing the fruit of Christian faith in learning to do good for others (3:8,14). They were self-centred churches. There was therefore a chasm in their Christian lives between what they said they believed and how they behaved. They professed the love of God, but in practice were caught in selfishness.

The background to selfishness

All of us fallen human beings are prone to selfishness, but on the island of Crete the problem presented itself in a particularly aggravated form (1:12). This happens where selfishness has gained respectability and has taken on the status of seeming to be the most logical way to live life. Where the philosophy of life underscores our innate egocentricity, there selfishness will be particularly exacerbated. It can take over the thinking of people in such a complete way that we become unaware of just how much it is influencing us. It becomes as natural to us as changing gear as we drive our cars. We do it without thinking. So a gap opens up in Christian living and people are blind as to why.

The ancient island of Crete was a place where a great civilization had arisen and had failed. Our post-modern Western civilization similarly sees itself as failing and in decline. Where a society's vision of itself and its future collapses people are left confused and disorientated. Ideals of justice, truth and love seem meaningless and impractical. This is fertile ground for a rampant subjectivism to take over. The whole of life is viewed, almost unconsciously, simply in terms of the question: 'How does this affect me?' Inevitably people are brought into the bondage of a deep and subtle self-centredness. And this affects Christians too, for the spirit of the age always rubs off on the church to some extent.

In such a society, to be idealistic is to be thought of as naïve. People have no common cause. The vision of the good of society as a whole is lost. The sanctity of personal choice is trumpeted, under the banner of self-fulfilment. Individual choice for personal well-being is perceived as the only true freedom. We live in such a culture. At best society can only be seen as a market-place and individuals as consumers. At worst it becomes a jungle of selfish exploitation, where human nature is left to pursue the sinful cravings of its innate fallenness to the full. 'They are detestable, disobedient, and unfit for doing anything good' (1:16).

Perhaps it was because Paul realized that, as the history of the world progressed and the different gods and idealistic visions of fallen humanity inevitably failed, the human spirit would turn in on itself in aggressive self-centredness that he wrote to Timothy, 'But mark this: There will be terrible times in the last days. People will be lovers of themselves ... lovers of pleasure rather than lovers of God' (2 Tim. 3:1-4).

Symptoms of a selfish church

As we read between the lines of Paul's instructions to Titus we can see many symptoms of the selfishness in the churches on Crete. Sadly, many of the same symptoms dominate the church today.

Christians who are dominated by a subjective view of reality come to church not to seek God and to pursue his worship. They approach the church with the attitude of 'What can God do for me?' They are interested in their own individual well-being before all else.

They have little or no sense of the greatness and glory of God. 'Godliness' is a God-centred attitude which pervades a person's life. There is little godliness (1:1) about their attitude. Instead of the church being a kind of solar system where people's lives orbit around Father, Son and Holy Spirit, one God, it is more like a bag of marbles where each one jostles with the other for attention and prominence. 'Nobody cares about me.' 'People are so insensitive to me.' These are the cries of the self-centred church. Under the surface there is malice and envy (3:3). The whole sense of serving God and doing good to one another has been lost (2:7).

The self-centred church is also a church where morals are lax. Self-centredness provides no encouragement to self-control or to say 'No' to worldly passions.

The self-centred church is also a church where family life is in disrepair. As husbands and wives pursue self-fulfilment at the expense of loving servanthood there is friction between the genders. Men forfeit their wives' respect (2:2). Women find their role in the home to be a burden rather than a blessing (2:5).

In particular the self-centred church is a sitting target for false teaching (1:10). True Christianity is not an easy road. It involves daily taking up the cross in the battle against sin, and daily denying self in the pursuit of loving service. The self-centred Christian (if he is a Christian at all) wants eternal salvation, but is desperately keen to find a less irksome path to heaven than the narrow way of following in the footsteps of the suffering Lord Jesus. False teachers are adept at making their message appear biblical (3:9), but at the same time trimming their preaching to appeal to our baser instincts. Their spirituality is all about success and feeling good, not about repentance and Christlikeness. The self-centred Christian is particularly susceptible to heresy.

The other side of this coin is that the self-centred church will seek to appoint as its leaders those who please men, rather than those who please God. Perhaps the congregation is prepared to offer large financial rewards (1:11) to those who are able to entertain them rather than challenge them. The self-centred church is a church which has lost sight of what is actually required in the character of a Christian leader.

It is a congregation which would rather hear interesting theories, mysterious stories or diverting anecdotes than sound biblical teaching (1:14). Its worship is about therapy for the congregation rather than the glory of God.

God's cure

Moses once asked God if he could see his glory. There is a sense in which that request was an impossible request. For no fallen, mortal man can look upon the face of God and live (Exod. 33:20). But by God's grace Paul had seen the glory of God in the face of Jesus Christ and had met the risen Lord on the road to Damascus. That sense of the awesomeness and greatness of the Lord was only underlined by the fact that Paul found the all-holy God to also be God our Saviour (1:3; 2:10,13; 3:4,6).

The cure for self-centred Christians is the truth about God our Saviour. This is the truth that leads to godliness (1:1). The

world does not revolve about us. There is a sovereign God who
works out all things according to the pleasure of his will, and
brings his elect to faith in his Son, the Lord Jesus, who 'gave
himself for us to redeem us from all wickedness and to purify
for himself a people that are his very own, eager to do what is
good' (2:14). The world is not ultimately a market-place of
human choice; it is the theatre in which God is working out the
purposes of his kingdom, through his servants. This is the
truth, which is still the truth whether it appeals to people or not.
This is the truth which calls for an attitude of reverence about
the way we live (2:3) and a tone of seriousness about the way
we speak (2:7).

The truth of God our Saviour exposes the subjective, self-
centred approach to life as a fatal mistake. It shows us first of
all that a world which pursues 'all kinds of passions and
pleasures' (3:3) is a world which is horribly 'enslaved' and in
need of rescue by God our Saviour. It shows us that a world
living in self-centred 'malice and envy' is a world which is
'deceived' (3:3), for if God gave himself in self-sacrifice in the
person of Jesus to rescue us, then to live a life of self-
indulgence is to prove that we do not know God (1:16).
Conversely, if we are the recipients of the grace of God in
having our sins forgiven through Christ (3:7), then the only
way we can seek to live without being hypocrites is to emulate
the 'kindness and love of God' (3:4), in lives of self-control,
godliness and works of kindness and goodness. Such lives
commend the gospel of God's grace to the world (2:10; 3:8).
God has generously poured out his Holy Spirit in order that our
lives might be thoroughly cleansed, renewed and empowered
to pursue such a course in life (3:5).

Wonderfully, God our Saviour gives eternal life to us
through faith in Christ (1:2). Self-centred attitudes are aggravated by loss of ideals and vision in a failing society. But
though all the civilizations of this world fade and prove
unsatisfactory, God calls his people to a life beyond this world.

In Christ we are people who live our lives with our eyes firmly fixed on the world to come, the return of Christ (2:13), which Paul calls 'the blessed hope' (1:2; 2:13; 3:7).

Here is a vision which banishes our despair. Here is a hope worth waiting and enduring for (2:2). Here is a kingdom worth working for. Here is a future worth pursuing. Here is the truth of the gospel which leads to godliness. Here is the grace of God which engenders a Christlike faith, love and self-control, which exposes the worldly self-centredness of the church for the vile and ugly hypocrisy which it is.

God is our Saviour. He loves us with an overwhelming love, which has appeared in our world in the life, death and resurrection of Jesus Christ. How can we but revere him with deepest worship? How can we but model our lives on his grace and live for his service? These things are not only to be taught in the church, but lived out before the church in the lives of Christian leaders, appointed for their blameless lives, their holding firmly to the trustworthy apostolic message and their ability to oversee God's church and inspire it to faithfulness to God our Saviour.

Appendix
Bringing Christ into the workplace

If the workplace is to be brought once again under the lordship of Christ, what are the obstacles which must be overcome? This is a vast subject which requires someone with greater experience and competence than mine. However, let me highlight three problems which it seems to me must be faced squarely, if Christians are truly to make a difference in commending Christ and Christian values to the business community.

1. Feelings of impotence

Business and commerce, with its underlying professionalism, is such a vast edifice. The rate of change, the sophistication and complexity of the modern workplace confront us as over-whelming. It is understandable that as we face the challenge of recapturing the workplace for Christ, we can feel impotent, and conclude that the task is totally impossible. We may agree that the aim of enthroning the Lord Jesus in the workplace is right and proper, but we are so small and the task so huge that it is ridiculous even to try to change things. We have to realize that that very attitude is an obstacle to making progress. Have we never heard of the story of David and Goliath? Yes, we are very small, but our God is bigger even than the multi-national giants of our day. In the name of the Lord Almighty, the living God, impossible battles can be won.

2. Erroneous ideas

There is a need, of course, to be realistic about the modern business world, but we should beware of adopting ways of thinking which tell us it is impossible for the Christian to make a difference. Back in the seventeenth century, the great Puritan Richard Baxter published his *Christian Directory, or a Sermon of Practical Theologic and Cases of Conscience*. In this tome Baxter addresses himself to the business world of his day. He takes as his starting-point the commercial environment of Restoration Britain, and his teaching is designed for 'Rome or London, not Fool's Paradise'. In particular, though, his attempt to formulate principles of economic conduct for the Christian implies that economics are a department of life for which each individual is morally responsible, and not the result of the impersonal mechanism of so-called market forces to which ethical judgements are irrelevant. The Christian, Baxter insists, is committed by his faith to God's standards, and these standards are as obligatory in the sphere of business transactions as any other province of life. To the popular objection that religion has nothing to do with business — that 'Every man will get as much as he can have and that *caveat emptor* is the only security' — he answers bluntly that this way of dealing is not for the Christian. What Baxter tries to do for the Christian businessman of the Restoration needs to be done again for the modern world.

3. Complacent attitudes

No doubt some Christians receiving this call to reform the business world will respond with: 'Things in the modern workplace are not so bad. Just stop worrying!' But even if this were true (upon which the seemingly endless news of business scandals in our day would cast doubt), we are still called to seek to make Jesus Lord in practice in all areas of life. Our ambition should be 'that in every way [we] make the teaching about God our Saviour attractive' (2:10). We are not called to complacency, but to seek to capture the spirit of the workplace for Christ.

This requires major initiatives on the part of Christians in business. It requires prayerful thought which the anti-intellectualism of much of present-day evangelicalism does not help. It requires that Christian Unions in businesses should become not just places for taking a spiritual hot-tub of 'fellowship' during the lunch hour, but the arenas where strategies for Christ in the business world are forged. This is an enormous subject and all I can do here is to seek to stimulate thinking in others. However, I do recommend the reading of a little booklet by Os Guiness entiled *Winning back the Soul of American Business* (Hourglass Publishers, Washington, D.C.).

Select Bibliography

D. Guthrie, *The Pastoral Epistles,* Tyndale Commentary, IVP.

Philip H. Towner, *1-2 Timothy & Titus,* IVP New Testament.

Philip Jensen & Tony Payne, *The Path to Godliness,* St Matthias Press.

Roy D. Clements, *Turning Points,* IVP, 1995.

J. C. Ryle, *Five Christian Reformers,* Banner of Truth.

David F. Wells, *God in the Wasteland,* IVP, 1994.

Graham Twelftree, *Drive Home the Point,* Monarch Publications, 1994.

David Seamans, *Healing Grace,* Scripture Press, 1989.

Brian Walsh, *Subversive Christianity,* Regius Press, 1992.

Os Guiness, *The Gravedigger File,* Hodder & Stoughton, 1983.

John Piper and Wayne Grudem, *Recovering Biblical Manhood and Womanhood,* Crossway Books, 1991.